118

GOTHAM
GIRL
INTERRUPTED

GOTHAM GIRL INTERRUPTED

My Misadventures in Motherhood, Love, and Epilepsy

Alisa Kennedy Jones

imagine!

An Imagine Book
Published by Charlesbridge
85 Main Street
Watertown, MA 02472
9617) 926-0329
www.imaginebooks.net

Library of Congress Cataloging-in-Publication Data available upon request.

ISBN 978-1-62354-534-5 (hardcover)
ISBN 978-1-62354-528-4 (paperback)
ISBN 978-1-63289-217-1 (ebook)

Interior design by Jeff Miller
Cover design by ConnieB/& Friends

Printed in the United States of America
10 9 8 7 6 5 4 3 2 1

To my two, Olivia and Sophie,

and to Ed,

I made up this interpretive dance

with a stick and a ribbon

just for you.

I sing the body electric,
The armies of those I love engirth me and I engirth them,
They will not let me off till I go with them, respond to them,
And discorrupt them, and charge them full with the charge
   of the soul.

—WALT WHITMAN

"Pull up your socks. Get over it."
—NORA EPHRON

. . . And their hairs stand on end to a shimmer of leaves
or the movement of clouds, and the way that the tense
has been thrown like a switch, where the land turns
to dreams. . . .

—PAUL FARLEY, "Electricity," a poem from
The Boy from the Chemist Is Here to See You

Contents

Introduction

HELLO FRIEND! Thank you for picking up this book or for borrowing it from some well-intentioned acquaintance. And thank *you*, well-intentioned acquaintance, for foisting it upon some unsuspecting reader!

In 2010, at the age of forty, I was diagnosed with a severe form of epilepsy. The cause was a mystery. What is epilepsy, you ask? Simply put, it's an overabundance of electricity in the brain. Less simply put, it's a serious chronic neurological disorder characterized by sudden, recurrent episodes of sensory disturbance, loss of consciousness, or convulsions, associated with atypical electrical activity levels in the brain. With more than forty different types of seizures, epilepsy affects sixty-five million people worldwide. Because of the complex nature of the brain, epilepsy can strike at any age and manifest differently depending on a variety of factors.

My seizures are the kind most often portrayed in the media, meaning the afflicted person falls to the ground and thrashes around until some brave-hearted Samaritan comes to the rescue. They're dramatic. I look totally possessed when my eyes roll back into my head. If I'd been born during any other era, I'd likely be institutionalized or burnt at the stake by some angry white guys. Over the years, I've had hundreds of seizures. They tend to involve four phases: the first is the *prodromal* phase, which means before the fever. This is the emotional or intuitive voice that whispers, "Some shit's about to go down." The second phase is the *aura*. Sometimes an aura can be as subtle as a shimmer of light at the edge of my field of vision. Other times, it's more hallucinogenic and has me asking, "Whoa, what kind of *Donnie Darko* movie is *this*?" Then, there's the third *ictal* phase—that's the seizure itself, the electrical storm in my brain where I'm usually on the ground in convulsions. To those around me, it may look agonizing but I'm actually not feeling any pain at this point—just a gorgeous black bliss. Lastly, comes the *post-ictal* phase where the convulsions have stopped and I'm out cold. In the moments when I'm regaining consciousness, I might be confused or frightened, but mostly I can really *only* focus on what's directly in front of me—often it's the smallest things.

Seizures tend to put one in a constant state of disaster preparedness. Picture a pilot fixing an airplane engine while it's flying or, in my case, as it's crashing. Some of the preparations I've made over the years might seem ridiculous, but then I've never claimed to be the most logical girl. Still, epilepsy is about having a plan, a "Here's what we're going to do . . ." and then improvising as things with the condition evolve.

People tend to think of epilepsy as something that primarily impacts children, but it can strike at any time, no matter how healthy you are. As with so many stigmatized chronic conditions, I tried to keep mine under the radar for years for fear that people might misjudge, mock, or withdraw. If I wasn't having seizures all the time, I reasoned, not everyone *had* to know.

Then, in 2015, I had "the big one" that nearly destroyed me, laid me flat and left me the most vulnerable I've ever been. It was brutal. It changed almost every aspect of my life, forcing me to start completely over from zero—I couldn't speak, eat, or work. I couldn't go out in public without frightening people. The experience led me to believe that people *do* need to know more about this condition and that perhaps they also needed a different narrative approach. I know I certainly did.

For years, I've called myself a spaz. Why? Because when you are a nerdy, too-tall, introverted, single girl-mom with chunky glasses, who has epilepsy, anxiety, and depression, at a certain point you want to take the derogative term back from the historically mean asshats of the world—primarily people who say epileptics are spastic freaks who are addicts, junkies, drunks, crazy, dangerous, deranged, possessed, demonic, divine, incontinent, unreliable, unable to hold down a job, unable to care for children, and so on.

Whether you have epilepsy or not, chances are you know someone who is affected by it. I happen to think we are *all* a little neurodiverse—meaning we are all uniquely neurologically wired. Where one person is the quintessential extroverted life-of-the-party, another is an introvert completely overwhelmed by people, chatter, and music. Everyone experiences the world according to her/his/their neurological makeup, and we shouldn't have to go around faking "normal" all the time.

Epilepsy is certainly not *all* that defines me, but it's also a thing that's not going away anytime soon. To go around hiding the fact is not only exhausting; it's totally missing out on the richness and hilarity that comes when we are all put together, as people, side by side and forced to understand and deal with difference. And I'm with Carrie Fisher on this one; I am constantly perplexed by the stigma attached to mental illness, the various chronic neurological conditions and the differently-abled. If you are walking (or rolling) around New York City or any town with epilepsy, living your life, connecting with people and able to feel compassion for friends, family, and your fellow humans, or to feel even slightly productive in your own right, you deserve a standing ovation—not a kick in the teeth.

We need to stop being such uptight weenies and admit that it's high time the world learns to adapt, make room for, and *embrace* all kinds of people along the spectrum of ability and neurodiversity instead of everyone always tiptoeing around topics of neurology, mental illness, autism, epilepsy, and so many other chronic conditions governed by our brains and genetics.

Over the years, people's questions about my conditions have ranged from "Do seizures hurt?" to "How come you're not completely developmentally delayed and/or traumatized?" More often than not, the questions are more a reflection of the person asking them than anything to do with me. My answers are typically, "No, my seizures don't hurt" and, "Actually, they can be quite beautiful." Indeed, some of the instances when I've felt most intellectually inspired, most human, and often most creative in my life happen when I fall, thrash around, and then get back up. For me, it's like the ultimate system reboot—a vibrant Technicolor awakening each time. I won't pretend that it isn't a doozy or not complicated, but my family (and Oprah) raised me to believe that my ideas, thoughts, and opinions mattered, that they were grounds for more inquiry, and that it's only when we are able to connect the dots between our deepest points of vulnerability and tell our stories that we can change things.

So, this is my story about *not* tiptoeing around the difficult dots. Little did I know (as I was writing this) how much the concept of neurodiversity would come to matter, the idea that whether you have anxiety, depression, addiction, bipolar disorder, autism, or epilepsy, the point is your own individual neural wiring might in fact be your magic rather than a tragedy, that it might allow for finding meaning in places you never expect it to and with people you'd never anticipate having in your life. Yes, you may be different; you may be in a chronic waltz to feel at home in your head or in your body. You may even feel trapped in there for a long stretch (as I was), but it doesn't make you less; it makes you magic.

That's what this book is about.

The one superpower epilepsy (or any chronic condition for that matter) *shouldn't* give you, however, is invisibility, so I wanted to write stories about loveable weirdos with all different types of wiring to ask, Why can't the awkward, spazzy nerd win after all? Why can't she/he/they end up with the good, funny, amazing person who is her/his/their own equal and opposite counterpart? What's to say they can't live out a truly great rom-com? Why can't they have a full tribe of kooky friends and family who have their back? Why can't they have a rich, rewarding career? Why, with technology, science, and modern medicine should there be any hindrance?

For my part, I have told these stories as I remember them, which means salted and peppered with truth and exaggeration, with names changed to protect the guilty and the innocent, starting with my parents. At times, it's more of a rescue-and-recovery operation than a memoir because I'm filling in certain blanks with reflections, bad ideas, and inappropriate metaphors. I wrote them in a kind of fever dream, my own series of seizures, a lightning-bolt flipbook of time-lapse photography on a hyperloop. Factor in a few grim flashbacks, select absurd hypotheses, and misunderstandings made funnier with prescription drugs, and there might be a book in it.

Epilepsy can lure you into powering down your whole self—especially your funny side—and I believe this is a mistake. Some things are out of my control. Others, well . . . let's just say are a self-made mess. Some are absurd. The breezy humor you find in this book may be a defense mechanism, but I believe it's a necessary one at times and an excellent self-care tool when you can tap into it. By taking a comedic approach to these stories, please know that there's never any intention to trivialize or diminish the suffering people experience as a result of epilepsy. It's a devastating condition, but we don't have to *stay* devastated.

Okay, time to get to your safe space, people. This is how it always begins. Here comes the shimmer . . .

1

"The Big One" (2015)

"**D**on't speak. It's going to be okay," he whispers.

Okay, sure. I don't have to talk at all. I'll do whatever you tell me because I am a really good student and . . . wait, where am I? I feel . . . wrung out like a dirty dishrag. And *who* is *this guy* standing over me? Well, hello, smoldering antihero! Mothertrucker, he's hot and his voice is so . . . swarthy?

"I want you to blink if you can understand me."

I close my eyes.

I open my eyes.

"Did you take something, Ms. Jones? Blink once for 'yes,' twice for 'no.'"

I try to shake my head "no" but I can't move. In fact, I can't feel anything. I think I'm strapped to one of those neck-spine boards they use to keep you from being paralyzed after an accident. For now, I can only look up at this man, whose hair is just stunning. So lustrous and thick, it's like a 1970s ultrashag carpet. You want to camp out on it and play Monopoly like a horny twelve-year-old at a slumber party.

Now, before we go any further, you should know it's practically a law in New York City and rom-coms everywhere, if at any point in your beautiful life you ever pass out (for whatever reason—hold on, I am about to explain), you *will* invariably be woken up by a handsome, scruffy firefighter or paramedic type, someone authentically brave and badass, with a deep voice and great hair—like this guy over me. Whether you've gotten black-out drunk and inadvertently slept with him, or say your brain decided to spontaneously combust in the grocery store, it *will* happen at least once. In my case, it's the latter scenario.

Still, the calculus of this exact moment, of waking up to an amazingly handsome man telling me to blink, isn't quite computing. For God's sake, I was just going for coffee. Wasn't I? Not fancy coffee made for me by some well-intentioned barista with piercings and a soul patch. No, for once, I was actually buying coffee *in a can* to make at home because I was doing like Suze Orman told me and putting my latte money where it might count someday: drugs. Lots and lots of drugs.

As I made my way down Eighty-Sixth Street on the Upper West Side of Manhattan, I reveled in what felt like the first real day of spring. The air held a clean crispness. Think iceberg lettuce in a wedge salad. The kind they still serve at old-school steakhouses named Kevin's or Ken's. Where only a week ago the winter of 2015 had been as frigid and grim as in *The Shining*, now the glass and gunmetal buildings glowed sunstruck. Everyone was smile-squinting. Yes, even the most curmudgeonly of New Yorkers do this. That old guy on the stoop next door who always smokes a cigar in his purple bowtie, even *he* was smile-squinting. It's like when the clouds part in Portland and everyone rushes outside for a fix of glorious vitamin D.

I slowed to bask in a warm, luxurious squint. I felt the muscles around my eyes scrunching up in the grin-worthy brightness. Shimmering fractals unfurled before me. To the west, a double note of thunder over New Jersey. Or had I imagined it? I've always been oddly sensitive to storms, but I felt good. Maybe a slight itch of fatigue? I had been pulling long hours at work lately. I felt a subterranean murmur, like the thrumming of bees in the back corner of my mind. My epilepsy—or more specifically, my *seizures*—often begin this way. Well, most of the time. There's the shimmer at the edge of my vision, the thrum and the thrash. Should I turn back? No. I wasn't going to have one today, I told myself, pressing on. Not today. I feel fine. *Just breathe, girly.*

Mostly, I was feeling righteous. After a productive morning working on a new creative campaign for a live televised super-hero takeover of the city, I'd survived hot yoga without being singled out by the teacher, Yogi Wallace, who somehow always managed to stupefy the class with his radiant smugness.

And yes, in that moment on the street, it might as well have been the opening credits to *Mary Tyler Moore* where she tosses her hat high up in the air just as you hear the theme song go, "You're gonna make it after all," because I *was* making it. After all.

I had gotten the best job in advertising a writer could get, making the most money of my entire adult life. Instead of navigating nomadically, job to job, from writing one bad TV crime pilot after another, I could finally afford to be alive without constant single-mother anxiety. The kind where you're always holding your breath at the checkout to see if the debit card clears. Finally, after years of scrambling, nose-to-stinky-grindstone, scraping to get by, sucking up to entertainment and tech-preneuer douchebags, who spoke almost exclusively in corporate synergism jargon interspersed with words like "hella" and "bro," I finally felt respected at my job.

3

I'd made the big move back to the East Coast for work, and so both my daughters could be nearer to their dad. The girls seemed happy. For the first time in years, they were finally going to have everything they needed. They weren't going to be the poor, broken-home kids that other parents pitied. They'd already been through too much in their short lives. Suffice it to say, I had made it through a feral divorce—a veritable blood sport of blame, self-recrimination, and dueling indictments. If you've ever been divorced, you'll immediately get this: it's the equivalent of waking up and being in a head-on car accident every day for about two years, complete with neck braces, scary forms, and even scarier attorneys. While I hadn't escaped completely unscathed, my hair still looked good, and my little blog, *Gotham Girl*, an ongoing love letter to New York City weirdos, was starting to find real traction. Plus, I hadn't had a seizure in almost a year. This was a big deal for me because as I mentioned earlier, my brain likes to blow a fuse (or all the fuses) now and then.

I'd spent five years trying to crack the code of epilepsy with different treatments, medications, diets, gurus, and whatnot. With each grand mal seizure, where I'd lose consciousness, drop to the ground, and convulse uncontrollably, my world became a near-constant obstacle course filled with sharp corners and hard edges. I'd awaken to crazy bumps, bruises, cuts, and concussions. Looming over me was an ever-changing cast of freaked-out strangers, prickly doctors, and loads of ambulances, bills, and consequences. But I'd solved it. The meds were finally working. *I* was working.

I was also in love. More love than I'd been in for what seemed like nine hundred thousand years, and I didn't want to jinx it. At this point, I'd probably qualified to have my virginity reinstated. His name was Loïc, short for Louis, and he was my exact kind of crazy: a good-quirky-smart-silly Frenchy. We laughed nonstop—at my very broken French, at his even more broken English, with ridiculous conversations where he would implore me, "Mon amour, why not just to use zee sugar cubes if you always get zee wrong amount of sugar in zee café every morning? It's plus exacte, non?"

Okay, yes, I was in love with Pepé Le Pew, but he was right; I *did* always grumble about putting the wrong amount of sugar in my coffee every morning, and these were *exactly* the kind of silly tête-à-têtes that I wanted to be having after all the years of struggle. Mostly, I could see us getting married one day in some handmade backyard ceremony in France—complete with Polaroids, ukulele music, and crafts that made the guests all feel mildly superior. I could feel a future weaving itself together like some richly patterned fabric.

I felt such long-legged joy as I walked into the grim little grocery store on the corner, only slightly bigger than a bodega. I was rocking my favorite jacket and my ever-present big bag, a Louis Vuitton Empreinte Citadine tote—a gift from an old squeeze—a terrible boyfriend but one with great taste in purses. To be clear, my big bag doesn't look terribly fancy at first glance, but it is. For all you nerd ladies out there, it's like Mary Poppins's carpetbag when she meets the kiddies for the first time. It holds everything: computers, baby wipes, extra shoes, subway reading, a built-in pharmacy, too much lipstick, and even its own wallet on a leather string so you never lose it. How smart is that? I swear, if this bag had running water and electricity, I'd probably live in it.

Still, as I made my way down the coffee aisle, I was overcome with a sense of satisfaction that had nothing whatsoever to do with accessories. I felt I'd finally become the person I'd always wanted to be: a solid person who wasn't totally failing at becoming a better person, who thought of others first, who paid all of her bills and all of her dues, who didn't let circumstance rule outcome *entirely*, who donated to public radio, who read *real* books, who showed up on time (more often than not), and one who'd let go of past gripes, grudges, and regrets.

Yes, I was finally figuring things out, and feeling pretty badass. Again, I shook off the hiss in my head, or was it the damn fluorescent tube lighting of the store? I couldn't tell, but just as I bent down for the can of Martinson Breakfast Blend coffee (smooth mild roast), the world fell away.

(My editor wants me to say here that *I* melted into the floor, but that's not actually how seizures work for me. There is no time and no feeling other than a buzzing in my head and sometimes maybe a tightening around my temples. But *I* don't melt into anything. Instead, it's the world that starts to shimmer, and *it* melts away in a swift vertical wash of slivering, slicing black cuts, like eyelashes blinking closed. Or eye*slashes*, as I call them. It's accompanied by a momentary feeling of exultation that, maybe, only I truly know, but still it's magnificent because it's a moment of pure, ecstatic joy.)

"Ms. Jones, *did* you take anything?"

Oh . . . you again. I tune back into the swarthy stranger above me now. If they were doling out middle school nicknames, his would simply be "The Hair." He reminds me of a pirate: a tidy, well-groomed pirate with perfect teeth, which now that I think about it, has to be spectacularly rare because everybody knows pirates never brush or floss. They're too busy looting. It's practically science.

I wish he would kiss me. For a second, he leans in closer and I think he might. Wait, no, I love someone. I love someone, don't

I? Where am I? Things shift, and he looks so sorry and sad, as if someone has just spanked a puppy. I feel instantly terrible for him. In my head, I can hear myself: "What's wrong, *Mr. Hair*?" Still, there is a heaviness now bearing down on him, and on me, a kind of reverse gravity. He seems physically pained, like his chest is about to cave in. I take in his shirt: there was a medical snake-cross-thingy on the pocket, and he is covered in blood and bits of something pinkish-gray. Oh man, is that my brain?

Wait . . . did I just get brain on hot-hair-guy? And wow, that's *a whole lot* of blood. That's pretty much a *Walking Dead* amount of blood. And then I realize; it's happened again. I've had another one—another seizure. That was the shimmer I felt. The thrum. The hiss.

As I lay there wishing my brain bits were back inside my head where they belong, I think, *holy crapdazzle* . . . isn't this just the absolute, foundational analogy for life? The moment you think you're the person you've always wanted to be, suddenly you're *not*. The world rushes in to compel you to become something *more*, something different, something *else*, because nature abhors a vacuum. Where there's a void, nature always seeks to fill it with some kind of form. And that really *is* science.

You may be wondering, is this how this person really thinks all the time? Even after a seizure? Or is it creative reimagining? The short answer is, this is pretty much how I process the world. Even in the middle of a crisis, I live in a state of constant reimagining, creative commentary, and improvisation. Plus, again, I've had loads of these. I've never been a huge fan of the survivor narrative. Inspiration porn isn't really my jam as not all suffering is redemptive or transformative. Some of it is just *hard* and majorly sucky. To generalize wildly for a moment, I think you take certain risks; you make yourself vulnerable to go after the thing you want. In the process, you fall, you thrash and flail around; maybe you get banged up, maybe even a little bloody, but then you get back up and press on. Just like a seizure. Fall, thrash around, get back up, and press on.

I can't really blink my answer to The Hair about having taken anything (mostly because I take *everything*), so I croak a whisper up to him as best I can, "I-nuh-staz . . ."

"A what?" he says, leaning down now as though I am whispering a code word for entry into a secret society.

I try again, "uh sppzzazzz . . ."

He cocks his head, looking quizzical. "A spaz?"

I close my eyes.

I open my eyes.

He suppresses a smile and says, "You've had a seizure." To his partner, a guy I can't quite see, he rattles off, "Status epilepticus . . . blah-blah-dee-blah-blah . . ." Everything sounds like molasses now. ". . . Dislocated jaw, compound facial, cranial, dental fractures and lacerations . . ."

Processing his words, all I can do is blink in a Morse code of my own making: *Good God, why couldn't I have fallen on my big bag instead of my face? What's the point of having a big bag if it doesn't at least function as a pillow or a helmet?*

Then he is back talking to me, trying to channel his most upbeat but sorry self: "There are things they can do . . . implants, prosthetics . . ."

Prosthetics? *Dear me*, prosthetic *what*? His words trail off again, and I can see him realizing that just before this moment, maybe only twenty minutes ago, I was probably a very different girl than I am now. And I just want to tell him, "Don't be sad, *hot-hair-ambulance guy*. This isn't my first brush with the electric."

2

Everything in New York
Is a Little Bit Broken

WHEN WE ARRIVED at the hospital, I was too afraid to look at myself. I avoided any and all reflective surfaces. I had no idea bones and teeth were technically poking through my face. Seriously, whatever you are imagining right now, I'm pretty sure it was worse. I just knew that everything about me was a little bit broken.

It's the same as when I try to explain New York City apartments to the rest of the developed world. People usually don't believe me. Don't get me wrong—I love my apartment. I love living on one not-so-level floor where marbles would roll back and forth by themselves and all my stuff is just right *there*. I confess to being a little absent-minded—especially on all the new drugs. But even before that, I once lost our hamster in our apartment for a week. She was fine, but only because I also lost a pizza.

The first thing I typically tell people is, "Look, you need to understand that everything in New York is a little bit broken." Every building has its quirks. Certain fireplaces only work on the third Thursday of every other month. There are windows that need a hard nudge in a particular direction in order to open depending on the weather. You practically have to be a master locksmith (and recite magic words) to get into the city's older apartments—it's all a little broken. In most prewar rentals, everything is retrofitted with clumsy renovations. Don't even get me started on the railroad apartment and how no one part of the house can be gotten to without going through the whole rest of the apartment, and privacy is for sissies, so get over it. And best of all, there is almost *always* a refrigerator problem.

Every single apartment that's even worth having in New York City—the one that has those built-in bookcases you've always wanted or perhaps it's in the perfect location right next to the dog run, *it almost always has a fridge problem.* The fridge is either too big or too small, or it juts out oddly into the space so that you stub your toe every time you walk by it. Worse still, some idiot renovator decides the main storage unit for all things edible in your life should go right next to the bathroom— or why stop there? Just put it *in* the bathroom right across from the toilet, or in the tub, if you are so lucky as to have one of those.

Now I too was broken—my face, jaw, and teeth to be exact— but no one in the ER seemed to know where to put me. I was still fading in and out of consciousness when The Hair solemnly took his leave.

Breaking your face is a lot like falling through pond ice. There's the initial shock of razor-slicing coldness cutting into every part of you and then, within what feels like seconds, there is a gradual slowing of all systems—circulatory, respiratory, digestive, and nervous—that takes hold. It's a prevailing still-ness. I felt my body temperature dropping, as I lay trapped beneath the frozen surface of my mug.

I knew from my obsessive Googling that there are more than four hundred miles of blood vessels in my brain alone—that didn't even include the face with all its tiny capillaries laid end to end. The bones in my face and jaw seemed to have cut sharp paths through them. My lower jaw had effectively been ripped off from the upper part and then broken through the bottom of my chin and through the left side of my face.

There had been no brilliant fireworks with this particular seizure, only obsidian darkness flooding in from all directions. In the cold depths where I was immobile and starved for oxygen and for an inner monolog, I tried for a millimeter of outward movement. I tried to wrap my lips and tongue around any sound I could try to make, but the word *help* with its "p" sound at the end and lips momentarily touching together was too difficult. The only sound that would come out was "hell . . ." It seemed appropriate for the moment.

Overhead and all around me, there was an orchestra of humanity that is the New York City ER department. I could hear the overly intimate moaning of other patients behind neighboring curtains while nonsensical wailing came from behind a closed door in the near distance. Meanwhile a psychiatric patient was yelling into a trash can. Nothing was okay that day. And it had to be okay that it was not okay, I told myself, hoping I'd fade back into my usual, velvety, postseizure blackness, but instead I was relentlessly awake. In my head, I could hear myself whispering, "I see live people."

One of the live people I saw was Rakesh. He was not ER staff or an EMT on a break. From the narrative fragments I picked up through the curtain separating our two ER bed bays, he was there for his son who had fallen off some dangerous play structure in the park and broken an arm or some other such bone.

11

They had taken away the kid for X-rays. Now this kind-looking, beautiful, brown-skinned man had spied me through a slit in the curtains. His face was one of horror upon making sense of me. He also made out that my whisper of "hell" was actually a call for "help" and came closer.

"Do you need me to get someone?" he whispered from a few cautious feet away.

I tried to nod yes, but wasn't sure if my movement could be discerned by the outside world. "Yes!" I yelled from inside my head. The pain was dull and distributed but still overpowering like a tidal wave bearing down on every bone in my body. He seemed to understand me and scurried off to find a doctor.

A few minutes later he returned. "They are coming," he whispered again, his expression still grave. Approaching closer now, he introduced himself in broken English. "My name is Rakesh. I am driving Uber. Would you like me to pray for you, my child?"

"Oh God, no!" I screamed inside my head. "Don't pray for *me*, Rakesh! Pray for morphine! Pray for *any* opioid pain relief!"

He put his hands out toward me now, both palms facing me as though he might lay them on me in some evangelical, holy roller prayer ritual, except I was probably still too bloody and gross to actually touch.

Oh no, where were the nurses, I wondered. Through the curtains I could see scrubs flitting past us now. There must be a shooting happening or a code blue. Jesus Christ, why wasn't *I* a code something?

Glancing up at what were surely moldy ceiling tiles, Rakesh closed his eyes and began to pray in hushed, melodious, Hindu-sounding tones. "Lord Jesus, we pray to you now for mercy. Please come into this poor, wretched . . ."

Wait, wretched? Who's wretched? Have you seen my purse?

"... suffering soul," he continued, voice rising in intensity. "And drive the devil out of her, most merciful God . . ."

Oh, for fuck sake.

"Cast out the demon of pain from your poor, wretched daughter, Lord . . ."

Demon of pain? Holy cats! No, just cast out the pain. Maybe cast in some Advil? I'll keep my demons, thank you very much, if only to do my bidding later.

Then, raising his hands, Rakesh started speaking in tongues, which I want to say went something like this, "Nnngyoooooo–tammmmmmmmm–yaaaaaaaaa–zahhhhhhhh."

Don't get me wrong. I was grateful for the intercession on my behalf since I couldn't speak, but inside my head and outside my head, I'd already been through enough. I didn't get any coffee that morning; I'd seen bits of my brain on a hot guy's shirt and then lost him for good. And somehow, there I was, still pleading, "Someone, just please, anyone . . . hit me in the throat with the back of a hammer, right now! Let me go back to my usual postseizure coma! I'm too tired for all this fanfare."

Just then, a nurse entered and Rakesh-the-exorcist stepped aside to let her get to my IV. "Are you saved, my child?" he asked before disappearing behind the curtain.

I am now, I thought, not entirely facetiously. Then, the black curtain of morphine came down on the scene, or was it another seizure? I couldn't tell. I didn't care. I was back to *not* being, which was fine considering the alternative.

I AWOKE SOME TIME LATER to a very tall white ghost at the end of my bed. It was my best friend, Ed. Ed is probably not quite tall enough to qualify for giants-only sleep-away camp, but because he is a commanding salt-and-pepper executive type, I think most people often mistake him for one. There's a waspy, I-rule-the-world, deep-voiced quality to Ed. And he is a total dead ringer for New York City's current mayor, which can be really funny when we're out walking together. He'll pretend to be the mayor and tell some poor tourist very sternly not to litter, or a speeding cabbie to slow the heck down when taking a left through a crosswalk. It's totally the best and slightly evil because people's eyes go all wide with false recognition and they immediately freak out and obey him on the spot. Then later, you might see a blurb in the daily Gotham news blotter, "Mayor D. tells littering hipster tourist to tidy up!"

I think the hospital was under a similar impression about Ed being the mayor because, while I'd been off in the great, glorious outback that is my unconscious brain, it had been a literal game of musical rooms, I later learned. I'd been in the ER, the OR, the X-ray, and what passed for a broom closet as well as a room with another patient named Alissa Jones who was having some random organ removed. And so Ed, my giant service beast—my service unicorn, as I call him—had been required to have a full-on, grown-up man tantrum and use his "mayor" voice to get me decent digs with a reduced chance of life-altering medical mistakes.

There'd been a stroke of luck, he also reported. The head of the maxillofacial surgery program had been in the hospital right as I had been brought in and had seemed very excited by how smashed up I was. It takes five hundred pounds of force to break the human skull with the thinnest part being near the temples. That's mass multiplied by acceleration. I am only a hundred and twenty pounds and had fallen but a short distance (two feet), so apparently I had done a real number on myself. They were coming soon to talk to me about next steps.

In the meantime, Ed was trying to distract me with the PBS series *Wolf Hall* playing on his laptop, which I thought was hilarious because I realized in my morphine-induced stupor that Ed is *also* Sir Thomas Cromwell. If you're not familiar with the history of the sixteenth-century British monarchy, fear not. Cromwell was King Henry VIII's right-hand man—a cunning idealist from the back streets of London—who masterminded Henry's divorce so Henry could not only get down with the hot strumpet Anne Boleyn but also undertake a heap of other nefarious things involving executions, torture, and the creation of the Church of England. In the fog of drugs and blinding pain, it was clear to me Ed was a total Cromwell and I was *so* the ne'er-do-well Henry VIII—but without the turkey leg. The point is, Ed always loves running back and forth amid all the different key players (neurologists, surgeons, nurses, and lunch ladies) trying to get everyone to agree and take action. It is his favorite thing in the world. He's like a more effective United Nations, only in giant human form.

Still, in the lead-up to my surgery, no one was agreeing. Apparently, the neurology team had decided to try me on a newer, stronger epilepsy drug, but I needed to stabilize on it before the maxillofacial team could begin the lengthy reconstruction of my face, because if I seized on the table during the operation, I could die. It turns out a sliver of a millimeter in the wrong direction while shaving a bit of bone near the brain might very well disfigure and/or paralyze you. A micron slip of the scalpel around the wrong blood vessel and you could easily wipe out a decade of memories. On the other face-bone side, it was complicated because we were in the "golden time," which I understood to be a short window of opportunity for operating on faces before super-intense swelling typically sets in. Call me naïve, but I never knew this was a thing. If they didn't operate soon, it might be another week before they had another opportunity. To each set of doctors, I was like a Jenga tower piled precariously high and set to an egg timer quickly running out of sand.

My face, nervous system, and basic bodily functions were all competing against each other for dominance on the chore chart. Again, I was caught in the middle of two decidedly not great options: (1) wait to stabilize and stay safely alive while risking being terribly disfigured and in the hospital for another two to three weeks, or (2) go for the gold during this "golden time" and risk seizing on the operating table while they put my face back together so that I might be the least deformed version of me in the long term. If you're anything like me, you are a girl, and underneath all of your emotional depth, you're still vain as fuck and so you go for option two. Do you really want to live out a super-long life as a poorly constructed Jenga tower?

The only thing you really wish for in a moment like this is to be able to time travel back to the instant right before the seizure. The moment on the street where you sensed *things* might go sideways and then you *actively choose to listen to your gut.* You turn back to the safety of home, your apartment with its overabundance of pillows and soft things, the place where you lose everyday items and yet you never lose that inner gut voice. More than anything, you wish you'd listened to it in that specific moment.

According to my girlfriend Holly (who showed up soon after I was brought in to support Ed and who is another, albeit much shorter, Cromwell-ian navigator), there was a great deal of arguing around my bed. You might think it was a clusterfuck of ineptitude, but I'd like to think it was mostly just people acting in good faith. I couldn't make out all the details, but it resembled one of those scenes from *Charlie Brown* where the teacher is speaking unintelligibly over the loudspeaker in a sort of *mwaw–mwaw–mwaw–mwaw–mwaaaaaaw* sound. Apparently, there was also a stretch of time where I would insist on sitting up absolutely straight in the hospital bed because I was in too much pain to recline even slightly. For once, I had ballet-perfect posture, which I never have because I spend most of my days hunched over a computer like an old crone or a mollusk. But there I was, oh-so-properly with my pen and paper, writing out my answers to the various doctor questions.

What I remember most tangibly was meeting Walter. At six foot six, now there was another giant in my life, except this one was the living, breathing incarnation of the late actor Walter Matthau. As the head of the hospital's maxillofacial surgery program, there was an almost wizard-like quality to him. He was like Gandalf or Albus Dumbledore. He seemed to give off his own curmudgeonly glow. Walter is not a man of many words, but when he does speak, it's the plain truth without any sugar-coating. There's a gravitas to everything he says, even when he's joking. Practicing for more than thirty years now, Walter is a specialist who handles New York City's worst cases: "the jumpers who lived."

There was something strangely comforting about Walter, the way he would study me and then the way I would study him back since I couldn't speak. We were like two orangutans checking each other for nits. I could tell he was a tinkerer, the kind of friend who came over to your house and took your whole car apart piece by piece for hours to identify the mystery problem, fix it, and then put it all back together late that night with infinite patience and specificity. He was the surgical equivalent of the guys from *Car Talk*. As he examined my jaw with its bones poking out through my face and my right eye rotated back into my head, he looked down at the giant binder of incident notes and said jauntily, "Oh, you're right in the neighborhood."

I was loopy on pain meds, which was how I was able to even communicate, but by this time I could nod a small "yes."

And then he said, "Ah kid, why couldn't you at least fall in Zabar's? Don't you know? Someone wouldda caught ya in that store?" And I laughed out loud, which hurt like a mother, not just physically but also because I usually *go* to Zabar's. Christ almighty, I would *live* in Zabar's if I could—right next to the cheese section. Still, I'd been trying to do like Suze Orman told me—get the cheap coffee. She owes me a serious latte.

The other doctor who figured into the goings-on was the consulting neurologist, Dr. Delia. I remember less of Delia as my brain was starting to do a funny thing at that point—whether it was the drugs or just straight-up trauma, I may never know— but it was collapsing all the faces of the people around me into only two faces that my brain could process and recognize. Everyone started to look like either my giant BFF Ed or my girl-friend Holly.

Delia—who was completely new on the scene—would be talking to me about my epilepsy, asking questions to which I was writing all the answers out on paper, but in place of Delia's face I could only see Holly's.

My brain was face swapping live people's faces like a social media filter. I was effectively the character from Oliver Sacks's story *The Man Who Mistook His Wife for a Hat*. This was a trip, since it's a bit like dissociative misidentification, which you see in mental illness, except that I very rationally understood this person in front of me to be who she was, Delia-the-neurologist. But my eyes didn't see things that way. They disagreed—to my eyes she was Holly. At one point, Delia leaned in close to me and said, "Tell me about your first seizure."

And even though I couldn't speak, because she had Holly's warm, kind face, I felt so comfortable. I wrote out on my piece of paper, "Now, that's a story . . ."

3

The Unbearable
Brightness of Being

Fade in: La-La Land . . .

No, not the celebrated movie musical. I'm referring more mundanely to the ruthlessly backbiting, cock-measuring place of Los Angeles itself. Anyone, even Carl Sagan's chipper ghost speaking directly from the bardo, will tell you that La-La Land is full of *star stuff*: star walks, star sightings, star*lets*, star makers, star fuckers, star comebacks, star charts, star doctors, star diets, star cleanses, and star dog walkers. You name it. Everywhere you look it's stars rising, flickering, shooting, falling, flailing, or fizzling. My first seizure there in 2010 only adds to this list of stars.

As I glanced in the rearview mirror, it was clear I was having a Gene Wilder morning. My hair was set to super-crazy static. Brushing it would be a no-go. I searched my dumpster of a mom-car for dry shampoo as the line at the drive-through Starbucks on the Santa Monica–Venice border came to a dead stop. Better, I resolved, to pat down the frizz with product and pretend the mess was 100 percent intended. Lazy French mom-look. *That* was the only way we were going to make it to the movie premiere on time. The other mothers of Santa Monica may have been all about three-hundred-dollar Brazilian blow-outs, but I'd already tried that and ended up looking like that poor, terrifying girl from *The Ring*. Besides, my world was *bigger* than my hair, I reasoned. I was a writer, not a performer. People were lucky if I showed up wearing any pants at all.

All brains light up in order to send messages from one cell to the next, but some days, it felt like my brain could power the whole city's electrical grid. Not literally. It was more like a crack-ling, energetic feeling in my head. My machine was "on." I'd have so many thoughts going at once, you could simply plug a USB charger into my ear and light up the town or download a few dozen new plot twists. You could power all the tuna-can Priuses and shiny Teslas on the 405 freeway. I don't mean to sound like a jerkwad—as if my brain were somehow the answer to the city's first-world problems. I only mean to say that long before I ever had a grand mal seizure, I was already a pint-sized, livewire lunatic.

I was an odd, skinny, little twerp of a child. Think Don Knotts with features all out of proportion. I had yet to grow into my enormous ears. My eyes and lips were too big for my elfin nose. I also operated at two distinct speeds: child-reading and child-wriggling. When I wasn't in a corner with my nose buried deep in a picture book, I was dancing. I would spin like a top, kicking, zinging, and gyrating in my pleated plaid skirt and dark blue knee socks.

I was especially demonstrative about my one true preschool love, American folk singer Jim Croce. Indeed, by age four, I was deeply smitten with the much older, much-mustachioed musi-cian. Yes, even as a child I loved the swarthy lads, especially the ones who didn't eat paste. To this end, you could often find me boogying fitfully in front of the hi-fi in my grandparents' living room. I was especially down with Croce's rousing classic "Bad, Bad Leroy Brown." In my mind, Jim was the ultimate stud. A poet but not a pretentious sissy, he was emotionally available to my four-year-old heart, yet still a badass.

My fidgeting wren of a mother, who was probably trying hard to behave under the stifling glare of her stoic Norse in-laws, would inhale sharply at my every move and wriggle as if to whisper-yell, "Stop the whirling for God's sake! You're going to break something!" By "something," she meant the collectible plates my grandmother had carefully, prudently mounted on the wall next to her vast collection of commemorative spoons. Though I did not yet have the verbal skills, in my head I thumbed my nose at the whole lot of them and shouted, "Impossible, you boring dummies! I'm bad, bad Leroy Brown! I'm going to break everything!"

That moment wasn't just the birth of a defiance that would become (ahem) a recurring theme in my life—it was also the first time I became conscious of what I call *the electric*. The second time, well, I blame free-range parenting. I better tell you what happened.

Once upon a time, there was a perfectly well-meaning hippie couple from San Francisco who suffered from chronic back-to-the-land fantasies of sustainable living. These were brought about by a steady diet of *Mother Earth–Nature* magazines and TV shows like *Little House on the Prairie*. Prairie, my ass. That show was shot in an LA suburb and everybody, including my wistfully crunchy parents, knew it. Alas, there we were, in the hinterlands of Northern California, looking at land just outside of Old Shasta, population 432. A once-thriving, now-creepy village, Old Shasta featured a post office, a greasy-spoon diner called Jay-Bird's that cooked almost exclusively with lard, and the one-and-only Jay's Market and Gas. All of this was owned by a beakish guy named Jay, who looked like a crook-necked cartoon buzzard. There were loads of trees and cows and horses— along with one extremely accessible, low-to-the-ground, unmarked, highly touchable electric fence. Made all the more inviting by the horse that was behind it.

What most likely saved my life: a pair of fantastically hideous shoes called Buster Browns. These were super thick, rubbersoled children's shoes that were very fashionable in the mid-1970s. You might as well have been wearing gigantic meatballs on your feet.

I was about ten yards from my parents when it happened. They had ventured eagerly ahead with their redheaded realtor, Janice, who was a churchgoing lady with springy, permed hair who resembled a bright orange toilet brush. As my father gazed out at the pastoral rolling hills that smelled like wet dirt and rotting flowers left sitting too long in the vase, he waxed poetic about things like beekeeping and organic root vegetables while my mother puffed skeptically on a True cigarette, her preferred brand, no doubt pretending she was California's "healthy" answer to the French. Meanwhile, I was busy dawdling by the horse.

Now, when you're a squat little runt of a kid, it's easy to feel like everything in the world is bigger than you, and there's a tendency to adopt the attitude where you're either afraid of all of it or afraid of none of it. I was the latter type of kid, and I was fascinated with horses. It's not just that they are completely beautiful, powerful, instinctive beasts capable of terrifying brute force, sudden strength, and lightning speed; it's more their faces I fixated on. Their great pooling, anime-style eyes always made them appear to me scared and confused. When I leaned forward, it was actually to convey in well-intentioned kid-speak, "Hey there, mister or missus horse, don't worry. My parents are completely chill, clueless agricultural poseurs who probably don't know a stitch about large animal husbandry and I'm pretty certain they won't make you do anything you're not super keen on . . ." and my index finger came to rest on the wire fence.

All of a sudden, SHAZAM! The bolt flew up my finger through my right arm. It was like being unzipped from the inside out . . . with fire! The current coursed through my kid-body, zigging past my tiny bird ribs, zagging down toward my little hoozie (causing me to pee just a teeny bit) and then it flew down my legs and shot my fully laced up Buster Browns clean off my feet. The next thing I knew, I'd been blown back and was lying flat in the dirt.

My parents turned to look back, their bucolic reverie harshly disrupted. I'm not sure if they were high, or if it was just the 1970s, but this was long before helicopter parenting where they always rush every child to the ER. I sat halfway up on my elbows, probably looking like a drunken midget passed out in the street. "Holy shit!" I would have said if I'd any inkling of the existence of such words.

"What on mother earth are you doing?" My father asked, puzzled. "Why'd you take off your shoes, kiddo?"

"But . . . err . . . I–I didn't take them off," I stammered in drunk midget-ese as my equally perplexed and exasperated mother struggled to put the dreaded meatballs back on and then brushed the sodden leaves from my hair. As I explained how I was merely *talking* to the horse when I touched the fence, I saw the jaws of my parents and their churchy realtor drop, aghast.

Their eyes widened just like the horse, and the toilet brush declared under her breath, "Lord Jesus!" as they realized I'd electrocuted myself.

"Didn't you *see* the sign for that said ELECTRIC FENCE?" they queried, shocked expressions all around, as if I was the one who'd lost my damn mind. This is when I reminded them that I was still only four and couldn't totally read big words yet.

"What's *eclectric* mean again?" I asked my mother who stood frozen in place, her cigarette burnt down to the filter between her lips.

Again, since it was the seventies, no one called 911. I never want to speak ill of people who were probably in their own unique way trying to give me an idyllic childhood, but I think my parents may have actually been the original, self-involved hipsters. From there on out, though, they were careful to relate very pronounced warnings right out of the blue. "If you happen upon an old refrigerator in a junk yard, never climb inside and shut the door." Or, "If you see a bowl of razors, don't stick your hand in it." (Hoo boy. This explains a lot.)

That night I couldn't sleep. My preschooler mind was whirring like a hummingbird, zipping from bloom to bloom and thought to thought. My head felt like root beer, its insides all fizzy and carbonated. I was coloring well beyond my bedtime with great fury as if the current were still alive on my fingertips. To make up for the midafternoon jolt, my parents bought me an elaborate farm diorama kit at Woolworth's, the kind where you had to color in all the grass and paper doll farm animals and outbuildings. It was some serious agrarian role-play complete with dangerously pointy farm implements. There was even white split-rail fencing to go around all the animals, which seemed to me ever so much better than the other kind I'd dealt

25

with earlier that day. No wonder that poor horse was terrified, I reasoned.

As I colored, I thought about the day, the horse, and the fence. I studied my zapped index finger and recalled the unzipping feeling inside of me. I'd been zapped, and I wondered now if I could make a zap now myself, or if maybe I was electric? I looked down at the chaotic pattern of my coloring, which seemed confused, as though the blades of grass were eddying in slow, swirling, perpetual motion. I couldn't stop coloring. I pressed the crayon harder to the paper, and I loved the feeling of it, an excitement welling up in me, my own charged particles swarming like fireflies in a jar.

Meanwhile, my father glowered in the doorway. "What are you still doing awake?"

Not looking up, I told him I was working, that farm life was a rough business and hadn't he seen *Little House on the Prairie*?

B ACK IN LA-LA LAND 2010, at the Starbucks drive-up window, I'd given up on finding the dry shampoo. I clung to my venti drip with 2 percent and inhaled so hard that were it not for the plastic sippy-cup lid, coffee would have spouted straight up my nose and scalded my brain. It was a sole moment of relief, of respite from life as a truly single mother—no boyfriend, no sex, zero personal life.

I was worried about how we were going to make ends meet on my writing. I have very few backup skills, other than writing pithy ad slogans and fart jokes. With zero alimony and very limited child support, our new financial reality was about to be grimly Dickensian. And as anyone will tell you, Hollywood is still a place where the primary interview question remains,

"So, how can you contribute to my greatness . . . or at least get me off right now, today?" I wasn't out of ideas. I was just well aware of the institutionalized gender nonsense that comes about when a too-nice nerd-girl tries to deliver them.

I'd known that well before I'd schlepped the kids out from the East Coast after my poor husband told me he could no longer take being responsible for my happiness. I'd spent most of my time since arriving in LA feeling exhausted and like I was failing. I never fit in with all the orange spray-tanned people. Yet, I'd managed to carve out a little life for us, with scraps of work, a handful of nonjudgmental friends, and family not too far away but also not too close. I went to yoga. I meditated. I waxed all the things I was supposed to—eyebrows, upper lip, chin, arms, legs, and hoozie. I ate and drank all the leafy greens the healthy people told me to. I told myself, no matter what, I *meant* well, even if Hollywood was making me seem *mean*, which is sometimes how you *have to seem* when you are out-numbered, undergroomed, and overwhelmed in LA.

My last script-doctoring job had ended more than a month ago, and with nothing significant on the horizon, I knew I was on borrowed time. I'd even begun to look at various corporate gigs back in advertising and marketing. I was in such a frenzy to nail down a gig, I'd been running everywhere, attending every coffee meet-up, every dinner party, and every lame networking boondoggle. I made the Kardashians look like shut-ins.

I tucked a wayward lock behind my ear, pulled out of Star-bucks, and turned south on Lincoln toward Venice. The fog was just burning off. It would be warm out today, probably near eighty, I thought, as I made my way toward our modest bunga-low in Venice. Driving along, I noticed the vision in my left eye begin to shift. All at once, the left side of the road ahead began to reel backward. The palm trees, shops, and parked cars shot away from me, as if I were driving in reverse. At the same time, in my right eye, the film of life began to speed forward at a pace faster than I thought I was driving. Everything in my right field of vision seemed to rush toward me and past me, accelerating. I felt a panicked hammering in my heart. What was happening? Did my bitter barista just roofie me? Everyone knows they're frustrated screenwriters. Which way was home again? Which way was I going? Was it north toward Santa Monica, or south toward Venice? I was just around the corner from home and had traveled this route thousands of times on the way to school, sports, and friends. Had I gotten turned around? I tried to catch my breath and pumped the brakes on our 1985 Mercedes surf wagon. Our tank of a family car had been restored and converted to run on veggie oil so you could fill it up with Wesson at Costco. I know what you're thinking: yes, I *was* my parents' child, but we loved this car. The only drawback was that anytime you went anywhere in it, you ended up smelling like a taco. I slowed the Wesson wagon to a crawl.

My eyes strained to reconcile the two films side by side, but it felt like a sudden shard—the exact *opposite* of a thought. Where, a second ago, there was nothing but road and trees and houses, now there was a small, certain darkness—a pinprick of a black hole growing in my consciousness. One I didn't want to see, know, or even think about right then. I tried to blink it away. I just needed the films to match up, but for a moment it was like a splinter of pure absence between them.

The angry blare of a car horn startled me back to life, the films merged before me in the driver's seat, and I was mostly back to normal. Yes, I was headed in the right direction. I just needed to get home, I told myself. I heaved a deep breath.

Breathing, breathing would get me back home. "Namaste, moth-erfuckers!" was my mantra. I just needed to drink more water and take an aspirin. "Stop being such a freakin' sissy," I scolded myself, using my inner mom voice and focusing on the road. I'd promised to take my youngest daughter and her friend Kasey to the premiere of *Nanny McPhee and the Big Bang* at the Television Academy. We'd planned to meet my friend Jacqueline and all go together. And I wasn't going to let work or money stress get in the way of a treat. Between the divorce and move, both of my daughters had been through enough in the last few years. This was one small thing I could *still* make happen.

At home, we were traipsing about. In. Out. Around. As usual, glitter was everywhere. For a ten-year-old going on thirty, Sophie was chirping away like a little cricket. Beyond excited, she was getting ready for approximately 109 minutes of Emma Thompson transforming from a warty old crone to a warm, magical, motherly being. I headed toward the car. As I called back to her from the kitchen, I felt a vague buzzing, like tiny electric needles in my temples, and an invisible metal band tightening around my head. My gaze stretched out across the kitchen to the driveway. And then as I stepped forward, the kitchen counter tilted sharply to the right. A black wash of paint flooded my vision from the top down, a dark watery curtain, a tidal wave of blackness falling on the stage of my life.

There was no time to react, to even put my hands out, or reach for anything to catch myself. Darkness is different from nothing. It's not that I see darkness in my head; I just don't see at all. The messages no longer flowed between body and brain. Not even a split second to notice or care that something was happening or had happened because there was no time any-more. No being; just a voluptuous, impenetrable blackness.

There was no distance, no distinction between it and me. I was as much part *of* the blackness as it was part of me. And that was okay. There was no pain. In fact, there was less than no pain. There wasn't even a concept of it because there was no "body" that I occupied at that point. No gravity. No corporeal heaviness—only nothingness but less than even that. Only light.

I'll have to check with the people who do science (like astrophysicists and such), but I feel like there is probably a very pragmatic reason for the speed of light. Complicated theories aside, we need light to take its time to get places, and fortunately, the universe is happy to oblige. Why? Because if you could see all the light in the universe, all at once, it would blind you in an instant.

What I saw was all the light in the universe, even the little bits you cannot see, a hundred thousand sparklers from a galaxy far, far away. Not entirely blinding but close. In it, I could feel the universe eddying like a fast-flowing river of stars. La-La Land and everything was illuminated—thank you, Jonathan Safran Foer. Like being trapped in the Van Gogh painting *Starry Night* in swift oceanic motion, but it was more than light. It was a feeling of transcendence, of unstoppable ecstasy, accompanied by divine chromatic effects: a rapturous, paradisiacal stillness and glow. Amid the rushing of countless points of white light, I felt myself wrestling blindly to separate myself from this luminous new inner geography, to get back from it and put words around it, to observe it. All I could get out or hear myself say was, "It's a lightning storm in my head." No deep, Jack Handy thoughts. Nothing profound. Just star stuff. It was unbearably bright and impossibly close, but still, I didn't want it to stop because it was beautiful. Ecstatic even. It was *the electric.*

Layers of voices slipped through the blackest blackness like sylphs enshrouding, swirling all around me, touching but not touching. I couldn't tell where they began and I ended. Was that my skin or hers, or whose? I had only the most fluid and flimsy of borders. I had the vague sense of dark blue authority, a uniform and possibly a badge. I have always had a problem with authority, and had I access to language just then, I might have said something impolitic like, "Don't tase me, bro' . . . I'm not one for self-diagnosis, but I think my brain might already be its own stun gun right now."

Later, shadows and hushed voices faded in and out, sounding like they were coming from a conversation down the hall in a vague middle distance of nowhere. Still only blackness, but one voice flitted past me. "She hasn't had a stroke," it said, and I couldn't tell if it was a man or a woman. Then, another shadow leaned in close, one that I could see only in a silhouette of black on white. I felt her velvety voice brush over me.

I knew this woman. She had been a mothering presence for my children and me for years now, a bonus mom. A costume designer for the movies and TV, Jacqueline had arrived in our lives by happenstance when I was working on a new pilot for a TV thriller. She always came complete with bags full of fabric, sparkles, glamor, and infinite patience for my children's cantankerous ways. She was the prize you found in the bottom of the cereal box—the kind of cereal your hippie mother wouldn't actually let you ever have because it had artificial everything in it. Jacqueline was her own Lucky Charm. And mine.

"Darling," she whispered now.

"Nanny McPhee?" I may have said back to her.

"Darling, you've had a seizure."

Now, I felt the gravity of my body being pulled down and out of the CT machine thing. I could sense the perfunctory comings and goings of medical people in blue and green scrubs. I recognized this feeling in me now. It was electric, like the fence.

"Good God, my brain is charcoal." I whispered.

Still, no nice doctor came to explain what had happened, or what a seizure was for that matter. It was a jam-packed Los Angeles ER. I was not diagnosed with anything. This wasn't an episode of *House* where a cranky middle-aged neurologist and his team of plucky residents work tirelessly to solve the medical mystery of why I'd had a seizure. I was released in Jacqueline's care with discharge instructions to follow up with a neurologist and take a bunch of pills that looked like horse tranquilizers.

It had all been unbearably bright and extremely close, but I was convinced it was a one-off.

4

Where the Hell Is
My White Light?

THE DAY AFTER that first seizure in 2010, I surveyed my prizefighter face. I sported an angry purple shiner, a cut lip, and a massive bump near my right temple where I'd cracked my head on the edge of the kitchen counter. I held a bag of frozen organic peas to my eye to ward off the swelling. I figured I could cover the shiner with sunglasses like the plastic surgery moms at school always did after their various procedures. Thankfully, I hadn't needed stitches in my lip. The scab was already healing and would fall off in a day or two. In the meantime, I would just look a tad diseased. "Just a touch of scurvy!" I could tell people. Nothing a little vitamin C and some water couldn't cure. Every muscle on or associated with my person ached to the point that simply taking a shower was excruciating. I wanted to take a bath but was told not to do so until I'd followed up with a neurologist.

More than anything, life felt strange and seismically unsettled. Out of nowhere, I recalled a conversation about God that I'd had with my father when I was a child. It went something like this:

"So, you're saying he's *everywhere*?" I asked.

"Pretty much," said my father from behind his newspaper at breakfast.

"And *no one* can see him?"

"Yep."

I didn't like it. Not one bit. What happened to mother earth? I must have been about five when I had this first conversation about religion with my dad. Other than their back-to-the-land nature fantasies and a love of Dean Martin Christmas carols, my parents weren't terribly religious people. Nonetheless, I was a spiritually inquisitive child. Heaven, I had already worked out on my own, was a cloudy white space in the sky where angels and good dead people hung out, while hell was a low-lying hot place for the baddies, but the idea of "God" was still a fairly abstract concept in my little kid brain. The world just seemed too big for only one guy to be in charge. This is why Santa had also seemed unrealistic to deliver all the presents. You'd need tens of thousands of minions—not just one guy and a couple elves, which is how he always showed up in cartoons.

"And God can see everything and everyone?" I persisted.

"Hmm-mmm," my dad confirmed, sipping his coffee all fatherly.

"Even when they're getting dressed?"

"Hmm-mmm."

"Well, I think he's a real perv." There was something annoyingly conniving about an all-seeing, omniscient being.

My father lowered his paper. "Where did you learn that word?"

"What word?"

"Perv," he persisted.

"*Columbo*?" I couldn't really remember, but I loved *Columbo* at the time because Peter Falk has always reminded me of a Muppet.

It was an early spiritual crisis, but I still think it's true; there is something perverse about God and the exercise we call consciousness. As I regained mine in the days following the seizure, I noticed I slept like the dead.

Now, home alone with the kids at school or at their dad's, what had happened with the seizure began to sink in and the stakes of it all felt unnervingly high. By the time I really woke up and my postseizure stupor had lifted, I felt a strange expansiveness in my head. An odd kind of floating. I started to wonder how close I'd really come to death. I had so many questions.

Thanks to pop-culture shows like fantastic 1970s paranormal classics such as *In Search of . . .* , narrated by none other than Leonard Nimoy, I was already all too familiar with the common trope of the near-death experience. "Don't go into the light!" you've no doubt jokingly shouted at a beloved television character or at your mate when he or she is on a raging emotional bender.

These NDEs (as the pros referred to them) always seemed to feature a single bright white light, perhaps at the end of a tunnel with gauzy angelic loved ones, all gently beckoning for you to cross over. And in most narratives, somehow if you don't cross over, it's because you have yet to fulfill your destiny or learn some lesson that aligns with your belief system. Maybe you even saw yourself from above during your NDE, on the operating table, or lying flat on your back in your kitchen.

In the quiet of the house, I naïvely Googled "grand mal seizure" and tearfully watched the videos of people writhing, their bodies juddering away in a hospital bed or on a soft couch only then to fall into a deep slumber afterward. The afflicted were usually attended to by a loved one or a couple of methodically calm but comforting nurses who had clearly seen this kind of thing all before.

I was unusually silent for me. Ordinarily, I am a gregarious Chatty Cathy and given to much cackling laughter and semi-melodramatic tirades, but not after this. This seizure had stopped my mouth in its tracks. I was mired in a deep swamp of ambient melancholy. I must have scared the hell out of my poor daughter. It had to be an isolated incident, I assured myself.

I kept having vivid flashbacks of the lightning storm that had struck in my head. The words don't really do justice to the electrifying dynamism I experienced during my seizure. It felt like my brain was actively reaching around inside my head, searching to fill in the blanks to reconstruct the memory of that day.

I realized there had been no single white light, no tunnel, and no overhead POV shots of me "seizing" on the kitchen floor. There had been no sign of my nanna or our old dog welcoming me to the afterlife. Where were all the beckoning loved ones?

I knew I had experienced a kind of "lights out," but what bothered me the most was that I didn't even know I was gone. What is so uncanny is that when something like this happens, you really don't miss yourself *at all*. And you think how can that be? But there *is* no you to do the thinking. You're just gone. I couldn't even miss my kids. There was simply no capacity for missing anyone while off in Seizure City, which meant I'd better get busy with missing them right away if that's how death was.

First there had been a gorgeous Van Gogh-esque lightning storm in my head that had felt so sublime, and then suddenly, there was absolutely nothing. Probably less than nothing because it was like blacking out, except with no brain activity whatsoever. Was this what it was like to be brain dead? Could it really be as ordinary and *bland* as all that? Was the end of life really just lights out? If so, I was going to be magnificently pissed off.

I noticed an odd openness. It felt as if I were standing in the middle of a great field with my brain having taken a deep, deep breath. Now there was all this new space. Buddhists sometimes refer to this sensation as having a *beginner's mind*—where everything seems new—as though you are seeing it for the first time. I'm not sure why it works that way. I'm sure there's some complicated neurochemical explanation, but I found myself often studying very small things such as the grains of coffee swirling in the French press coffeepot or the microfine pattern of dust on a window. My linguistic skills were also lagging, but the thoughts in my head were crackling like bacon in a hot pan.

If I had experienced a glimpse of the afterlife—apart from the pre-spaz glitter bomb—it seemed a bit mundane. No God? No heaven? Where were all the people? Where were my nanna and Jim Croce? Shouldn't he be there? And what of Princess Di? What about reincarnation? Where was the multiverse as semi-promised by the string theory nerds? And what about ghosts? I'd been *so* totally looking forward to at least haunting a few of the jerkier people in my life—moving a picture, stacking some chairs, and saying "boo!" Forget the angelic beings you might have heard about. This afterlife was more like when you actively try to remember back to the time *before* you were born and you can't because you're just *not*. It was very unsatisfying. I don't know about you, but I'd expected just a little more creativity from the universe.

As I brooded over the narratives about God—at least in the western hemisphere—it seemed the story went that God is always all powerful, all knowing, and all good. But if you took a look around at all the evidence—things like global famine, childhood cancer, evil dictators, tsunamis, and seizures—it seemed clear that God was either not all powerful or *not* all good. What was the use of that? But what had I expected, really? Santa? Fairies? Even a higher plane of consciousness would have been nice. I was taken aback by my own naïvety. Had I been such a closeted faithaholic this whole time, silently indulging in Anne Lamott's three essential prayers of *Help*, *Thanks*, and *Wow*? Those words we all whisper during life's inexplicable events?

To grow up in California is to grow up with a patchwork system of beliefs. The afterlife and God might very well be a big nothing, so you hedge your bets with *spirituality* and hope it's all worth it. Now I found myself challenged to even defend the "s" word. It was an existential conundrum, the banality of it all. I was disappointed.

Of faith and religion, Christopher Hitchens once wrote, "Faith is the surrender of the mind, it's the surrender of reason, and it's the surrender of the only thing that makes us different from other animals. It's our need to believe and to surrender our skepticism and our reason, our yearning to discard that and put all our trust or faith in someone or something. That is the sinister thing to me. Out of all the virtues, all the supposed virtues, faith must be the most overrated."

In the wake of my divorce, I had needed a placebo: literally anything to believe in and make myself feel better. Neuroscience hypothesizes that when it comes to brain activity, emotional pain looks a lot like physical pain. Bad breakup? Have a sugar pill and feel amazing. It turns out whatever you firmly believe in will actually make you feel better.

Naturally, I chose something super complicated to believe in, something that would elevate my sense of purpose. After all, didn't someone somewhere on TV once say that the moral high ground has quite a lovely view? I chose Catholicism. It fit all my requirements:

1. I wanted to feel righteous and rightness. I was devastated by the end of my marriage, and I was not going to do what Nora Ephron tells us all to do when she says, "You are not your divorce." I was going to persist in being an idiot and own the fuck out of it and out of martyrdom. Catholics are great at that, I reckoned. I fit the bill.

2. I also wanted a boyfriend, one with a moral compass stronger than all the other boys I'd known in life, one who had the same sense of soul-crushing guilt I'd learned from the Irish phalanx of my family. Plus, I was terrified of being outnumbered by the kids. Chances were a Catholic lad would exercise a degree of compassion toward my children, as he would have grown up with heaps of siblings and so wouldn't be terrified of my sassy, heathen daughters as other childless rubes might be.

3. I wanted a religion that partied. Go communion wine! I wanted dinner parties with amazing food, an earthy Cabernet Franc, and marathon conversations like the kind I'd had when I was married. The kind of dinners that ended with all candles melted down to the nub and geraniums wilting somewhere on a porch.

4. I also wanted a Thomas Merton approach to belief. Merton was this very cool Catholic monk who managed to harmonize

aspects of Buddhism and meditation with all the glorious guilt and neurosis of the Catholic Church. I wanted a little God but without all the dogma, if that makes sense. I certainly didn't believe in any of that *Secret* nonsense, which was all the rage in LA at the time, especially with their scary sweating rituals. Pass. I already had hip-hop yoga for that part of my day. In the end, Saint Monica's was only a few blocks away and seemed a perfect fit for my little spiritual walkabout. It worked for a time.

Up until my first seizure in 2010, I was the healthiest person I knew. No surgeries. No chronic anything except sadness after the divorce. Nary even a head cold! To be honest, I'd been spending so much time trying to live my best life in earnest with kale juice, mindfulness, and yoga, I hadn't given much thought to mortality—except that maybe after single motherhood, death might feel like a well-deserved nap? What was I supposed to do with this grim Hitchens confirmation? The idea that it was just lights out gnawed at me. Faith wasn't just overrated, it was a completely sinister ruse. I couldn't make sense of what I'd seen and felt during that first seizure. Was the big white light all just some neurochemical hallucination—an acid trip of the brain's own making? If so, did it serve any kind of adaptive evolutionary purpose? Maybe it provided much-needed distraction in the middle of dying. Maybe it was our brains' own way of coping with the transition from being alive to being dead?

I started reading different accounts of seizures and NDEs. I came upon this passage by Dostoyevsky who had recorded more than one hundred of his own seizures over the course of two decades: "The air was filled with a big noise and I tried to move. I felt the heaven was going down upon the earth, and that it had engulfed me. I have really touched God. He came into me myself; yes, God exists, I cried. You all, healthy people, have no idea what joy that joy is which we epileptics experience the second before a seizure."

I recognized this! This same split-second joy, these words, and this ecstatic feeling right before my first seizure, had it been a glimpse of God? Still, there was all the inky blackness and the void to reconcile. It bothered me. They say a bee's brain contains roughly a million neurons. By comparison, human brains contain about one hundred billion. The idea of neurodiversity holds that there is profound value in how each and every individual's brain is wired. Was I wired for a flash of the divine now and then? One so bright, it knocked me flat? I tended to think I was no more special than a bee. Still, I was irritated because I expected the universe to be slightly more creative than just lights out. *Thwack*, you're dead, you poor, dumb but very environmentally necessary bee.

The betrayal I'd felt during my first seizure was one of utter disconnection—a disconnection from a hope of more or a story of *more*. Hope takes a crapload of work and narrative invention to maintain. Hope can often be easier to hang onto in stories than in everyday life. Stories of origin, reckoning, salvation, and redemption reside much more easily with hope than the practical daily requirements of food, clothing, and shelter. These things take so much energy on their own I wondered if hope was even worth the trouble.

The flip side to hope, faith, and God suddenly feeling like *a big nothing* was that all at once, life started to feel like *a big everything*. If this was all you got, this one, single life, then there's *a big everything* out there to experience, so best to love, fail, take risks, make crazy-ass mistakes, and do what gives you joy because all you have is now. I know it sounds self-help-ish and obviously "YOLO," but coupled with my scary seizure, it was oddly freeing. Suddenly, I had permission to do whatever the fuck I wanted.

I'd grown up to become a fairly obedient but neurotic white girl. I'd wanted to believe in everything: Gods—new and old, the Buddha, witches, the tooth fairy, ghosts, cosmic justice, specialty causes like Hobos for snow leopards, and nice, non-probing aliens like E.T. I liked the idea of the unseen world and all its secret powers and invisible mechanics. I'd always loved that there's a "possible" out there, but the inscrutability and uncertainty of "God's plan" was so damn annoying.

Interpretation is how we batten down the hatches and secure the storm of our experiences. We tend to reach for any fixed point that might anchor us. I badly needed a mooring after the first seizure. *I wanted my goddamn white light.*

Writing had always been a mooring for me. When my big life failures left me with a bleak but unflinching skepticism that there is no God, no cosmic point to human beings, I could frame that disappointment with a story, or at the very least a joke. Everybody suffered, and once you figured that out, and only when you dropped the whiney questions like, why is this happening to me? could the more interesting questions such as, what makes joy? be asked and partly answered.

Still, all those hours and years wasted after the divorce. All those Monday-night adult classes I took to become a good Catholic, learning the books of the Bible and the Lord's Prayer, never mind dealing with communion, not swearing, and being less morally jerky. If nothing really mattered, not even what people think about you or how you made them feel when you're just *gone*, why be good? Why hold back?

Go ahead, read Ayn Rand and *be* a complete shithead. Eat, drink, and smoke what you want; tell those asshole kids to get off your lawn. Live every day like a Russian oligarch. The universe *doesn't* really have your back, so screw that hipster nonsense. The universe has a very low balance in its fuck account. And if anything, it's saving those dwindling fucks for Mother Teresa and the Dalai Lama. I never knew that Thoreau was an asshole until that *New Yorker* article 150 years after his death. All this time I just thought he was an admirable hermit. Didn't Nietzsche say morality is just part of the herd instinct anyway? Who wants to be a damn goat? I suppose you could be a lamb or sheep. They're more adorable, but damn if they don't get slaughtered a lot.

But it's not as simple as all that. Thinking about Ayn and Nietzsche, it's hard to have your gratitude toward God or the universe for the good things you have in your life *not* curdle into resentment. My personal theology was turning out to have more inconsistencies and plot holes than a sci-fi movie made by twelve-year-olds running around the yard with their iPhone 8s.

Was it Max Planck, the Nobel Prize–winning physicist, who said, "When you change the way you look at things, the things you look at change"? I can't remember, but I believe there were three big tectonic shifts that needed to happen in my person:

1. I probably needed to rewrite my point of view and unlearn a number of small certitudes that signified I was an adult and actually in charge of anything. I hadn't been in charge that morning of my first seizure. I had no control over my brain that day, so I shouldn't feel too terribly bad about it.
2. I also needed to go back to being a student. When you're a student, you actively seek to have your paradigms challenged,

dismantled, and even smashed now and then. You want to be wrong. You want criticism more than ever because you worry more about learning than about what other people think of you. My whole paradigm for parenting and the perfectibility of our children had gone out the window with the divorce. But if dying in my kitchen in plain view of my kid wasn't a good enough excuse for living, I didn't know what was. I needed to be okay with not being okay and learning things as though I never knew them to begin with—which was (conveniently) how I felt after this first seizure—like a beginner. Like a student.

3. I would need to stay funny, and in my postseizure crisis of faith, I realized something about the whole white light phenomenon that Leonard Nimoy was always harping on. It wasn't *a* white light. It was white lights *plural*. That's what I was seeing: a pointillist conspiracy of a million white lights, that tornado of stars I'd been caught in, that was my white light. And the strange religiosity I felt in the wake of my seizure had also been experienced by Joan of Arc and St. Teresa of Avila—thanks Google. But those ladies hadn't fared too well, so a sense of humor seemed both highly appropriate and necessary.

I also wasn't afraid of death (as much) anymore—whether or not it was a mere neurochemical process or a passage to a divine realm. Don't get me wrong, I was still very much afraid of pain and suffering, but more than anything, my seizure left me curious about the brain. And I confess, I *did* feel a kind of yearning to flirt with the moment that we perish. I didn't want to go there again or have another episode anytime *too* soon, but what was it that St. Augustine said? "Lord, make me good . . . but not yet."

5

Angry Mothertrucker

FUCK. I was lost . . . and things were a mess.

What do mothers do when there's a mess? They clean up. They straighten. They vacuum. (I *love* my Dyson!) Mothers know the life-changing value of "the reset." On film and TV sets, it's the same deal. You're always telling the cast and crew after a botched take, "Okay, everybody safely back to one!" which means everybody grab your props and get back into position, and let's try it all again. Similarly, my whole world had been reset. With every new seizure, the scene was suddenly filled with deadly sharp corners and even harder edges. All our modern furniture was a concussion risk that needed to be foam padded. I wasn't allowed to drive—which is probably for the best. With little to no sense of direction and a periodically tenuous grasp of reality, I wouldn't want me on the road either. I couldn't swim and there would also be no more hot yoga. I couldn't even cook a normal dinner on the stove as I might seize and set myself or the house on fire. Sigh. By age forty-two, I was supposed to baby-proof our home all over again, but this time I was the baby.

I know it probably sounds inconsistent, but I had such a palpable distrust of my brain, my memory, my sanity, and my body to even just stay standing upright. And for a writer, I became a wildly unreliable narrator. I was always on edge that I would seize again.

Worst of all, I had scared the crap out of my brave, little, resourceful, smarty-pants kid, and I had no idea how to make up for it. My ten-year-old regarded me now with fear. Her face, not yet even spotted with adolescence, conveyed worry and a premature maternal wounded-ness that left me insisting, "Hello, I am *still* the mother here!" I agonized that her heart had been broken too soon in life—by the divorce and now by epilepsy. If I dropped anything in the kitchen or the bathroom, a dish, or a hairbrush, she'd immediately call out from the next room in this stricken voice that, as a parent, just hollows out your ribcage. It's this telepathic/telekinetic sense of your child's heart and your own heart both darkening and caving in on themselves in unison.

The shrinks all say that children are constantly changing, disappearing overnight and then resurfacing as entirely different people each day. New moods, new cells, and even changeling character traits appear in the span of twenty-four hours that served their resilience. Still, a child should never have to worry about whether her parent is all right. I needed to protect both girls from whatever this was or wasn't.

So, I decided right then and there, *I would lie about the whole seizure thing.* I was going to be a big, fat, skinny liar. I would lie to my colleagues, to the other mothers, to my family, to my ex-husband, and to the FedEx guy. No one would be served by the minutiae of maybes and fears that this little neurological event of mine might stir up.

Like many before me, denial would continue to be my core strategy until I had a lock on what was really going on with my brain. This would give the girls and me not only time to process but also some much-needed privacy. The divorce had never afforded us this luxury. It felt entirely too public with the cast of rotating attorneys and disclosures and "ding dong, the bitch is dead." There's always a bad guy in every split—even in no-fault states. (Raises hand. Yes, it's me. I'm the snarky, vitriolic, wicked bitch of the west. What can I say? We'd built a whole life together. I didn't want to get divorced.) So, the privacy and safety we'd known before things all fell apart had been a warm bath. I needed that more than ever postseizure.

Denial of my diagnosis would also give me a chance to figure out an "upside" to all of the guilt I was feeling. It had found its way deep down into my Cracker Jack subconscious. There had to be a prize at the bottom of all that sugary goodness and I wasn't leaving without it.

If there is one great equalizer across all mothers of all 'hoods, of all socioeconomic backgrounds, ethnicities, cultures, religions, and ambitions, it's guilt. There are whole industries built around it. You could make a veritable wheel of it like the chore charts your mom used to hang on the fridge that said things like "Empty the dishwasher," but this chart would top them all. Guilt, over both the sacred and the profane aspects of motherhood, is a universal force—like gravity or dark matter.

Let's start with the profane things I might have said as my little sea monkeys sallied forth from my uterus and out into the cold, cruel dystopian world. They say you forget the pain, but really you don't. It might have gone a little like this: "Oh my fucking God, you fucking [insert cruel descriptor for husband], *you* did this to me, you fucking fuckwad!"

Or, since it was a teaching hospital, there was a group of young, terrified residents in attendance, there might also have been a little of this: "Why the fuck are *all of you* standing at the end of the bed cheering for my va-jay-jay? And I don't care if you're learning—you, on the end there, stop looking so horrified! You too, [insert expletive for husband's name]. And *no* rearview mirrors! Who the fuck *ever* thought *that* was a good idea?"

Or, if things weren't going exactly according to plan with the epidural I'd requested, there might also be some: "Oh, fuck . . . please, please, just push her back in and then please, please, give me a fucking C-Section!" (Repeats string of nonsensical expletives, knowing all the while the guilt is just a rain check arriving later, COD.)

Then, there were the wishes, prayers, and pleadings that happened in those last moments before she was out that might have gone something like this: "Oh fuck, I wasn't made for this! And *how* is our daughter not going to end up with a corncob head? Lord, please don't let her have a corncob head, or worse, a corncob brain, and even if she is corncobby in any way, shape, or form, don't let me be so shallow that I still don't find her completely exquisite. Oh, fuck!"

Then, "Good grief, her head is the circumference of hipster artisanal bologna! What if my poor hoozie stays like this forever? What if I lack the appropriate prostaglandins to make things normal again? Oh fuck, please God, or Gaia, or whoever the hell's in charge anywhere, just *get her out* of me! And pretty please, can I please, please just *not* poo on the table in front of all of these nice people?"

But from the moment you gaze down at their goopy little heads, that's when the sacred takes over and you realize what you've known all along: you are going to be apologizing to your child in advance for the rest of your life for all the things that will invariably go wrong. For all the little awkward and terrifying moments to come, you *know* you need an overarching damage waiver to protect all parties involved.

Even in your arms right then, you know that the extra-crispy hospital blanket is not *nearly* soft enough for their perfect, little Winston Churchill cheeks. And then, you realize that, way before this moment, there are all these instances coming in the future that you are going to need to account for as well—like when you make the wrong call at the class campout when her wrist is really fractured but instead you *believe* that one doctor-dad who says it's just a sprain and so no reason to cut the trip short. We're all just renting this life, so it just feels like you need to inspect it for dings, dents, and scratches before getting too far down the road.

In my case, with my elder daughter, Olivia, I'd been dilated to five centimeters for a good four weeks before going into labor. I'd hoped this hadn't been hard on her. Honestly, it was like walking around New York with my purse just wide open! Who knows what could have gotten up in there? Or she could have just rolled right out down Broadway.

As I beheld her perfect little noncorncob head in those first moments after delivery, it also occurred to me that I needed to completely *apologize* for eating all those off-limits unpasteurized cheeses and sushi that I'd had before I'd even known I was pregnant. Or the immense volume of salt I'd ingested because I had constant terror-based dyspepsia for all nine months that only things like salt and vinegar potato chips and greasy bacon could remedy. I definitely needed to apologize for that.

I said a sheepish "I'm sorry" and thanked my then-husband for not letting me name the baby after the anesthesiologist who had slipped me some eleventh-hour good stuff. For once, my husband had stuck to a plan. I also apologized for throwing a handful of tampons at the same poor man after labor number two. They'd bounced off his forehead. Nevertheless, he didn't deserve that. He'd been trying to find me sour apple Jolly Ranchers and other lady items anywhere near the hospital.

Another pie slice in the sacred wheel of maternal guilt, besides pie itself, was breastfeeding. I know people always describe breastfeeding as this beautiful, private moment between mother and child, but for me, there was nothing private about it. It was deeply and unbendingly public.

From the very first moment in the hospital when the nurse remarked that I didn't have very *latchable* nipples (What are those anyway?), breastfeeding was an all-access, live-streaming titty fest. I could have streamed it live on Twitter and it would have been more exclusive.

My daughters were both gigantic babies. They might well have been born lumberjacks complete with flannel—in case you couldn't tell from the number of f-bombs I dropped earlier in this chapter. At eight and a half pounds each, they had voracious appetites. And as much as I wanted to be an overachiever in this realm of motherhood with all the other smug, self-satisfied moms in their fucking Eileen Fisher blouses and their Boppy pillows, my body just couldn't keep up with the little ladies. I tried everything, but it was neither natural nor easy. Yes, there are whole industries designed to make you feel shitty about this one particular slice of motherhood. I'm not whining for a participation ribbon, but I don't think any mom should ever be made to feel guilty for supplementing with a little formula—be it SimilInfalackiform for your little one or Prozinaxipro for you because your hormones are on Mr. Toad's Wild Ride. Breastfeeding's not a foot race. And even if it were, there'd be no one right way to run it. It's more like a dance marathon, and sometimes you will have to change up your moves.

Nevertheless, you say to yourself and to your wee one while they're still gloppy in your arms, "Okay little person, we're not going to know if I'm a good parent for another oh . . . thirty-odd years, and even then people with solid parents and totally happy childhoods have their issues. You might really get irritated with me during the teen years. Or you could turn out to be a complete wastrel, but I am going to love you regardless and we're just going to try to keep things interesting so that life always holds some curiosity and joy.

I hereby commit all future earnings to the swear jar. I promise out loud not to be one of those annoying moms who give out boxes of raisins for Halloween. It's going to be all chocolate, all the time. And no cheap candy-corn filler. I promise to give you the Heimlich maneuver should you ever accidentally choke on a Tiddly Wink when you are twelve and long past the ages of doing such silly things. And if your little heart is ever broken by anyone, any boy, any girl, or any circumstance, I promise to stand up for you like a lioness and help put things back together and comfort you. If you are ever lost, I promise to come find you—even if you are lost in Antarctica and I don't like the cold. And even if I'm bad at boundaries, I'll do my best to stay back so you can forge your own path. I promise if I ever get to the end of my tether, to give myself a time-out (possibly with some Xanax). I will try not to embarrass you at too many school functions, except I *will* probably make big signs for sporting events that say things like "Go Dragons!" and cheer louder than all the other parents to the point where, from the basketball court, you tell me to sit back down and shut up. I promise to support whatever dreams you end up having even if they seem like long shots and as long as they don't involve too many tattoos because needles are sucky and you might change your mind about your various life narratives over time. Because this is the sacred long game, I whisper to my cheeky monkeys. It's where you come to grips with the fact that any truly worthy, long game is made up of many, many shorter games, scrimmages, and adventures. It's like an epic Broadway show with multiple musical interludes, different story arcs, unsavory characters, mean girls, meaner moms, unexpected heroes, rap battles, and a twist or two that none of us saw coming. There will, of course, be some poignant, happy-resolution montages coupled with farcical missteps, some offscreen quibbles, downright *Fight Club* scenes, and inter-missions, so we just need to pace ourselves; am I right?

To give a little more context I wasn't just a mindful parent; I was a manic one. I was so worried about my daughters' lives not turning out totally great. I'm the crazy mother who drove 1,800 miles from New York to Disney World in a blizzard so that her daughters could ride in teacups. I wouldn't recommend it to anyone else or do it again—although, we *did* have the Magic Kingdom almost entirely to ourselves, which was great. There were no lines to the rides because of the flurry of can-cellations, we had free run of the hotel, and we got to meet all the princesses. I was a feisty mother and I wasn't going to let the fucking universe with its shitty winter weather ruin my kids' jolly holiday. Sometimes the universe screwing with you feels personal and so you have to defy it. Did I need to do that again now?

After both births, I'd said I was sorry to the girls, in advance, for all the confusion that was about to ensue, but I never antic-ipated having to apologize for seizures or the anxiety, depres-sion, and consequences they would bring.

Even with becoming a mother, I'd hoped to retain a sliver of myself. It felt selfish but necessary. Sleep deprived with scarcely a minute to feel the hot droplets of a shower on my face, I was desperate to save any small piece of "the-me-before-them," to remember my most favorite words and expressions like *perspicacity* or *journey proud*, to be able to complete at least one single thought from start to finish, or to come up with a moderately creative idea. With every pressure that parenthood brings, it would be easy to become a shrieking dishrag of a woman if I didn't try to preserve some fragments of the chick I'd grown up with.

Still, the sense of guilt that gripped me on a molecular level after that first seizure was a doozy. The single thing to which my unconscious mind resolved was, "I'm sorry." I still have no memory of it, but when Jacqueline arrived at our house with the ambulance in tow, Sophie, my younger daughter, had helped me to bed. Apparently, all I kept repeating as I clung to her was how sorry I was. I couldn't stop apologizing—even in the middle of a grand mal seizure, with a concussion, a black eye, and a bloody lip, I was just so sorry. If I could have uttered it softly into a tin can and sealed it, preserved for all of her lifetime, I would have.

I'd always imagined better for her, for all of us. When you have children there is an unspoken agreement that you won't die on them, at least for a stretch of meaningful time; even if you *secretly* wish for it in a fleeting moment, this is mostly just a desperate wish for sleep.

In the days after my first seizure, I'd decided that this little "event" was an isolated incident. I had been simply doing too much hip-hop yoga, not drinking enough water, and stressing out about having no ideas for any wretched new reality shows that would surely write themselves if we just cast them with horrible enough people. It was one of those moments where I'd decided that I was not going to let this seizure thing *become* a thing.

Still, I was in this awkward place of not knowing what I didn't know. I had always been a healthy person—a tad high strung and neurotic but healthy. My friend Helene and I would do wheatgrass shots after booty class until we were completely high on wellness. I drank overpriced Kombucha teas. I meditated. I was doing all the right things—on paper and in practice. I'd even worked on a raw-food cookbook project—a mistake of incredibly farty proportions. But the seizure shook me. Healthy people always suspect the sick: she wasn't looking after herself, or she wasn't eating right, or she must have been drinking. All of the above had been true at different times of my adult life—but not lately.

And I didn't know what I really wanted to know *yet*. Before my diagnosis, I'd come home from the hospital and simply Googled the word "seizure," which came up as *an electrical discharge in the brain presenting in a variety of forms.*

As I read on, it felt like there was a whole laundry list of new rules and trauma-prevention factors to consider now. If you've never witnessed someone having a grand mal seizure, it definitely breaks all the *mom contracts*. Like crying at your desk at work. If you really want to terrify people around you, a grand mal seizure has the same effect.

There are two parts to the grand mal or tonic-clonic seizures that I tend to have. The first part is the *tonic* moment where all your muscles stiffen and air being forced past your vocal cords causes a sharp cry or scream. At that point, you typically lose consciousness and fall to the floor. You might bite your tongue or the inside of your cheek. After the tonic phase, the *clonic* part kicks in. With this bit, your arms and legs begin to jerk and spasm rapidly, sometimes bending and relaxing at the elbows, hips, and knees. If you are having trouble breathing from vomiting or if the seizure lasts too long, your face might turn blue. As the body again relaxes, you might lose control of your bladder or bowel. It's frightening even for the initiated.

For my part, I've been told I shake in spasms, all the while opening my mouth like an anaconda unhinging its jaw and making the frightening noises of a Japanese horror masterpiece. Yes, it sounds terrible, but just to paint a picture of how I roll, there it is.

Oh motherhood, it's a protracted state of conflict. You're never enough at work. You're never enough for your mate. You're never enough for your kids. I've never done big, scary drugs other than the ones that are mass-produced by pharmaceutical companies, but I'm told meth makes you feel like such a confident, laser-focused badass. Like you can manage everything with a satisfying, effortless brilliance. Suddenly your life is a spectacular performance art piece. You can lift refrigerators with your pinky finger. Above all, you are finally *enough*. I can understand wanting this feeling. My seizure had made me feel so much worse than being not *enough*. And I was still in denial about the whole thing. I was stuck at the corner of guilt and shame.

They say that if you experience guilt, it's a sign that you hold yourself to a higher set of expectations or standards and that with shame it's the opposite. I can't speak for other mothers and their modes of self-care, but I'm going to throw off the philosophical straitjacket here and say that I feel guilt because I *do* want things to be better. I want tuned-in but not helicopter parenting for my kids; I always wanted a stable home in one place and an interesting life for them. One where they could have it all, whatever "all" turned out to be for them. Guilt doesn't paralyze me; it propels me.

My guilt doesn't stem from any deep-seated kernel of unworthiness. I have always believed in myself the way I believe in my daughters. I was raised in the age of Enjoli. For the uninitiated, Enjoli was the iconic drugstore perfume of the late seventies and early eighties. Ten-year-old little girls everywhere grew up singing the jingle into a hairbrush like an anthem in their bedrooms with the male voiceover coming on at the end to say "the eight-hour perfume for the twenty-four-hour woman." It stood for second-wave feminism that said a woman could and *should* have it all—from the boardroom to the bedroom. But damn if it wasn't overwhelming.

I also came of age with books like *Women Who Run with the Wolves*. They had been part of the feminist canon under which I'd grown up, so I had embraced a certain amount of my own mischief and acting out to get by. Nothing too extreme—mostly just general mouthiness.

The more I thought about how our world might explode with uncertainty because of my seizure, the more it sank in: I'll take the wheel of guilt and wanting things to be better over the wheel of shame any day. I reject the latter wheel and chore chart—wholeheartedly and unreservedly. Motherhood is so fraught with ambition, desire, and socially unacceptable appetites, it creates these currents that women so often struggle to quell or channel just to stay functional and survive. Maybe the upside of guilt is guilt. Owning it, taking care of oneself in the face of it, and then letting it go: maybe with meds, maybe with mischief, and maybe with other mothers. If anything, what my seizure made me realize is that forgiveness was key in the face of the cultural, social, educational, pharmacological, industrial maternal guilt complex. The myth that you're somehow not enough because you might be a sick mother was horseshit.

Maybe I was not so lost after all.

6

Oh, the Pie-rony . . .

I DON'T KNOW ABOUT YOU, but when a crisis hits, I am often knocked back by the unexpected vastness of *the ordinary*. Like finding a perfectly formed paper clip in the twisted metal wreckage of a plane crash, it can be something as insignificant as an everyday household word. In this case, the word was *garage*.

In those initial days home after my first seizure, yes, I was felled by a *noun*, not even a verb. I'd attempt to say the word *garage* and instead the word *yard* would burst forth. In my head, I knew I meant to make the sounds that make up the word *ga-rage*, but they just weren't there. A second later, the word *garbage* would trip off my tongue and only after that would I get to *garage*. It was as though I could physically feel a set of invisible hands inside my brain kneading through different words and actions like a big ball of dough.

Not only was my word retrieval way off, my brain still felt like I'd tried to vape the sun. Everything was too bright—the daylight, darkness, my shoes. The motion of life felt like driving in a very fast car or like being pummeled in the face by an action movie that unfurls so quickly your eyes can barely keep pace with all the cuts.

"Why is the world shouting, again?" I'd ask the kids. The sound of life in all its forms was just too loud. Even the little beings, like snails and crickets, proved deafening. I'd also morphed into what would later be described as an unpresidential word salad. I was a panhandler for words for common things like coffee cup, Scotch tape, and socks. My inner monolog was set on pause or the tape had gotten snagged in the reels.

There were moments where I'd be completely fine but then falter. "Just put the plates in the . . . *thing* where you put the dishes before putting them in the thing that washes them," I'd tell my daughter.

"You mean *the sink*?" she'd say, giving me the side eye.

"*Sink*? Are you pranking me? Is that really a word?"

"Yes." Cue look of ten-year-old alarm. "*Sink* is a word, Mom."

"Huh, well, I'm going to look that up, missy."

It was exhausting work that had me saying all the wrong things and doing all the wrong things out of order and backward, and only realizing it after with a kind of uneasy chagrin. I'd put my clothes on inside out. Pants were impossible. I'd brush my teeth and then squeeze out the toothpaste after rinsing the brush. Can we roll that tape again? I'd search my head for the right words. I *knew* they were there, I could sense them like hidden books on the shelves of my mind, but I had no retrieval power. With each mental grab, my hand would pass right over the correct phantom volume only to miss it. I'd read that temporary cognitive delays after a seizure were fairly common, but it was unsettling.

I'd been given a supply of antiseizure drugs with vague instructions not to stop taking them, which given my hippie upbringing, clearly meant don't even *start* taking them. I didn't want to feel any foggier than I already did. Plus, pharmacological continuity marketing was not my bailiwick. I told myself, there was nothing really wrong with me. My seizure had been a one-off after all. An aberration. I'd probably been overtired or dehydrated. It wasn't hubris so much as a low-lying fog of fear creeping in close to the ground.

I don't think I had a full understanding of my brain injury at the time. Not only was my language off, so too was my execution and sequencing. I was continually getting things wrong like thinking of the object that is a spoon and going over to get one in the totally wrong part of the kitchen—all while knowing full well that spoons were in the silverware drawer on the opposite end of the room. I couldn't tell anyone about this as it might impact the girls—especially Sophie because she'd already seen enough action during the seizure itself. How could she ever *not* be scarred by it? I had to at least pretend I knew what I was doing or laugh it off—if actually caught in the act of being wrong or seeming ridiculous.

I'd combed through other similar cases online during my more coherent moments. There would be these sessions between a speech therapist and a stroke patient dealing with expressive aphasia. The therapist might ask the patient to say the word *chair* and the patient would respond with *table*. The therapist might then say, "Great, let's try it once more. Can you say the word *chair*?" The patient might falter and repeat the word, "Table. Table. Table!" and then start to sob out of sheer frustration, because he knows what he needs to say, but he simply can't say it. He can remember the days of the week, sing "For He's a Jolly Good Fellow," and count to a hundred, but he still can't say a simple word like *chair*. I recognized this.

I had never dealt with postseizure cognitive impairments before, but while Sophie was at school and Olivia was at her dad's, I opted to close all the blinds and settled on the Food Network for my convalescence. Ina Garten had the lovely, warm, soft-spoken voice I needed right then. Just the way she pronounced *bruschetta* felt like a comfy cashmere sweater. And there were no huge surprises in her world. Her husband, Jeffrey, was nearly always away, and someone safe yet pleasantly new would come over for lunch or an early dinner that involved mashed savory bread puddings and pork chops. I also found another comfort cook in Giada De Laurentiis, who tended to glow like her whole person had been routinely dipped in extra virgin olive oil, which seemed like a good idea postseizure. Giada also pronounced all her words as though she was chewing al dente pasta, which I thought might also help my still slightly slurred enunciation.

Anyone who knows me at all will tell you that my worldview is based almost entirely on food. What's a worldview, you ask? It's what you do when you're alone in a room and you think no one is looking. That's a worldview. I believe with my whole being that the world doesn't need a wall to keep people out as much as it needs a sandwich to a build bridge between them. If everyone in the world were made to try each other's sandwiches—even if they just took small, polite "thank you" portions of each one, there might be a tiny bit of peace on earth. In the country of *me*, my sandwich is a BLT—on sourdough with the bacon almost cremated and crunched-up potato chips and Russian dressing on it. Every culture has its preferred specialty—whether it is a hero or a gyro—and there would be a lot more understanding and empathy among people if they only partook.

The same goes for pie. Every culture has its own rendition of pie. A pie, like a sandwich, has a story. Invented by the Egyptians, pie has a whole narrative arc, a sequence that involves death, comfort, and healing. Did you know the piecrust used to be called the coffin because it was, in fact, shaped much like one? At this stage of my recovery, I wanted only to crawl inside the comfort of a crust and fruit and fat. I had been doing flashcards and singing sentences that's sometimes recommended for stroke patients, but in the end, I decided (alongside Ina) that if I had a problem with my brain, speech, and my literal pie hole (aka my mouth), I was going to cure it with pie. There are two pies I led with—one because it's easy, the other because it's fabulous. There was something about having to read (which was also a tad tricky at the time) and follow each step in the instructions, having to use my hands, and walking to different locations in the kitchen that would trip me up but then also *wake* me up. The more I did with my hands, rolling out the dough, peeling fruit, the more my words came rushing back. Words like *temperamental, lawnmower, parsimonious,* and *grappling hook.* (Grappling hook?)

This was how I would get my brain back. I'd cooked a ton when my husband left me and it had been a palliative. I decided I was not afraid to get baking wrong until I got things right. Oh, the sins I committed in the name of pie and words would put many a baker to shame—especially those darlings in the UK. I am of the mind, like numerous others before me, that when you grow up without much in the way of organized religion, you tend to make up religion everywhere you go. Given my worldview, I'm of the mind that pie *saves.* And now with the seizure, I'd planned to make a cult out of it. Its warm, buttery flakiness coupled with its filling in all the delicate sweet and savory forms is a living manifestation of comfort and generosity. Marcel Proust's *In Search of Lost Time*, which I confess to never having finished due to my own lost time, goes on for forty-some pages about the nostalgic power of a cake-like cookie. Well, here's where I go on for mercifully fewer pages about the restorative power of pie to rekindle words, executive function, memories, scents, and people.

The easy pie I started with was a pear pie with Gruyère baked into the crust. I'd originally happened upon it while watching the short-lived but much-loved TV series *Pushing Daisies*. I'd fallen in love with the idea of this pie mostly because it seemed so unexpected, which was how I felt overall at the time. Plus, in the show, the hero brings his one true love back to life with an electric touch of his finger, which was also pretty much how I'd felt after the seizure. I had been zapped back to life but now was profoundly worried underneath all my shameless pretending and fibbing that things were fine. I needed an easy pie win.

I ended up rechristening my pear pie the "Cheater's Pie" because our dishwasher was broken at the time. Can I just tell you how sick I am of intelligent design? Our dishwasher is not smart; it is fucking confused and neurotic, all of which meant I had to cheat whenever I could with ready-made ingredients like peeled pears in jars and frozen crusts. Still, the extra chore of doing anything sequence-based with my hands, including the dishes, was what I felt I *needed* to do to get speaking properly again.

The best thing about the pear pie is that while it keeps for about three days, it tends to be gone in two: once for dessert and once for breakfast the next morning. It's a great breakfast pie because the Gruyere in the crust keeps it from being too sweet.

But back to being a spaz . . . One of the most marvelous contributions of modern neuroscience is the concept of neuroplasticity. The idea that we can edit, revise, and interpret the stories our brains tell about our lives—even when we are bound or constrained by objective facts. I saw my job during these first days home from the hospital as one of working with my own head and nervous system to rewrite this recent story in a more interesting and productive way. If anything, after my first grand mal seizure, my neurological wires were crossed. The messages my brain was sending to my mouth and the rest of my body were confused, frequently lost, or going down the wrong neural pathway with the wrong set of instructions. But because of the notion of brain plasticity I could, by trying different things—making pies, singing opera, or learning a new skill like tap dancing—rebuild and even reconfigure the neural pathways in my brain to not only regain function but also forge new ways of thinking altogether. Out of chaos, I wondered if maybe I could make a new order and slightly different narrative for what had happened. I wasn't sure what exactly; it definitely had to involve Ina.

As I worked, I began to relearn where the different kitchen utensils were located. I regained my sense of sequence. There was A, B, C, D, but I began to be able to change things up with intent—rather than by accident. The pear pie gave me back old words like *sink*, *preposterous*, *cantaloupe*, *sentient*, and *juxtapose*.

The second pie I practiced rewriting my neural pathways with was a crumb-top bourbon cherry pie. (It's a tiny bit of bourbon, but I find it makes all the difference, though as a word of caution, most doctors recommend limiting alcohol when it comes to seizures. Except at this point in the story I didn't know any of this.)

While I'd be squishing the chilled butter into the oat and brown sugar mixture with my fingertips to make the crumb topping, I'd practice naming simple objects around the kitchen and singing songs I'd sung to the girls when they were little. "Many moons ago, in a far-off place lived a handsome prince with a gloomy face . . . for he did not have a bride . . ." The neighbors must have thought I was bonkers, but with the cherries coated in bourbon-sugar-orangey goodness and the juices bubbling up through the deep golden crumb top, it was magic.

What I love about this pie is the immense feeling of potentiality that comes with it. The scent alone is a wildly generous neurochemical "Yes!" to life. The first forkful is a massive "Fuck, yeah!" in your mouth. No wonder Queen Elizabeth I loved it so much. It is a moment of *total-beautiful-possible* that helped bring back words like *pusillanimous*, *vigorous*, and *Christmas*.

I made it a number of times before I got it right, but each time the story of the seizure and what had happened to me shifted a little in my mind. Sequencing came back: underwear, *then* pants. Gradually over the weeks there were beginnings, middles, and ends to different activities. Certain actions regained a familiar arc. I knew where the spoons were once more. I could say the word *dishwasher*.

So what exactly does *baking* have to do with word retrieval and sequencing, you ask? Absolutely nothing. I could have done any new or unfamiliar activity like sewing or painting and it would have helped my cognitive function. Why? Because my brain was building new neural pathways. Again, this idea of neuroplasticity—that the brain's ability to reorganize itself by forming new neural connections throughout life means that our brains can compensate for disease or injury and adjust their activities in response to new situations and changes in environment.

I N MY TEDX TALK about creativity, electricity, and the brain, I spoke about pie and about how *our brain's ultimate evolutionary function and most important job is to tell stories* and send messages—no matter whether it's to your big toe, to other humans, or to inanimate dessert ingredients. I've been trying to work this point in, but in a way that didn't go full meta on your ass or sound too heady. (Sorry, I just couldn't resist the puns.) See, my words are working again already!

7

D-day

THE NEUROLOGY WING of the hospital was on a high floor—
some twenty stories up. I'd postponed the recommended
follow-up appointment with the neurologist for three months.
From everything I'd read online, seizures nearly always signaled
something bad, something *serial* as our nanny Teodora used
to say when she actually meant the word "serious." A seizure
could indicate any number of serial things: a tumor, a stroke,
cancer, a brain injury, or something worse—something lengthy
and degenerative.

I tend to think the real medical examination starts in the
waiting room—with the nurse evaluating your penmanship on
the forms. There are always far too many of them to fill out.
Then, it's about magazine selection. No *Neurology Today*s in this
waiting room. Everything on the coffee table seemed specifically curated to take one's mind off of the brain.

Apart from the man reading *Marie Claire* in the corner with
his head wrapped up like a mummy, I could have easily been at
the manicurist. And all these people with brain troubles were
trying so hard not to look at each other. I picked up a copy of
Knitting Monthly. I have always been a terrible knitter. Lots of

dropped stitches, zero attention to detail. That's so me, I chuckled nervously to myself.

The seizure I'd had in my kitchen had been an aberration, I continued to tell myself as I perused scarf patterns for idiots. If someone could just loosen the bolt in my temple, I'd be fine. That said, what if my brainwaves indicated that I was absolutely bonkers? The worst thing would be for my ex-husband to finally acquire the hard evidence he needed to prove I was nuts.

What if they made me pee in a cup and all that came out was chardonnay, cigarette smoke, and extract of bacon? (I'd gone on a date the night before and we'd had all those things at dinner.)

As I covertly watched the other patients hobble in as their names were called, I realized it was yet another subtle waiting-room test of neuro-typicality and reminded myself to check my gait and balance when they called my name. No weird arm swinging. Stand up straight. Wings together. No sleepy pins-and-needles legs. Thank God I'd worn flats.

The child in me wanted a prize for even showing up at all. By subjecting my brain to a series of lie-detector tests, I was "adulting" for a change. I usually saved all of my responsible juice for the kids, so this was a magnanimous act of self-care I'd decided to perform on the day before my forty-first birthday.

"IS THIS GOING TO screw with my blowout?" I teased the pimply, moon-faced technician.

I don't know why, but I couldn't take the moment seriously. Probably because it felt all too serious. We were two nerdy strangers crammed into this gray little closet of a room. It was the kind of forced intimacy that recalled the sweat-inducing middle school party game Seven Minutes of Heaven. I was having an electroencephalogram (an EEG), which is a test that measures the electrical activity of your brain. Special sensors called electrodes are attached to your head. The electrodes are connected by loads of wires to a computer that captures your brain's internal electrical weather system live, on-screen, and as a scrolling printout. The tech was sifting through my tangled mane attaching wires to my scalp with dabs of cold, gelatinous glop.

I felt oddly giddy. I'd never had an EEG before (as far as I could remember), and I could only imagine that my mapped-out brainwaves would resemble a piece of Cy Twombly modern art: well-intentioned, faux-juvenile chaos.

"Ummm . . ." The tech seemed to turn my blowout question over in his head, but also out loud, "Not sure. It's a conductive paste that helps the electrodes adhere, so a little, maybe? It's washable, though."

"Fine." I sighed, rolling my eyes, blowout be damned. "I'm not a blowout kind of girl anyway. I always wake up looking like Eraserhead the day after the salon. Honestly, how *did* women in the 1950s survive without product and handheld hairdryers?" I babble when nervous, and I was a little nervous.

Still, I was practicing being a quasi-fearless, responsible grown-up by actively participating. I'd even taken the bus, which alone would make any sensible person tense, all the pressure of possibly having a brain problem before, during, or after ultra-snail-paced public transportation.

I had a big presentation back at the office in an hour and couldn't be late. My boss already didn't like me. I annoyed her with my general weepy incompetence and total lack of decorum. I should have taken a personal day, but that never worked with Clarissa. She had big abandonment issues. The good thing is that her hair was always terrible too, so maybe all this EEG glop would work in my favor today, I reasoned silently on the table. I could easily miss a whole year of work just doing my hair. It takes forever, it's so unruly.

"We also need to tape you up." The tech held up a roll of thick white medical tape.

"Sounds kinky." I quipped. He feigned a laugh, taking pity on me for a moment. My guess was that he'd heard lots of bad, nervous jokes in his time and probably been instructed not to react too pointedly to anything.

What was supposed to be a benign exercise in adulting was starting to feel like a surreal game of medical BDSM. The tech continued his careful ministrations to my head. I could feel him holding his breath now, brow crumpled as he attached each electrode one by one. He seemed so serious. Why did people have to always role-play so stridently?

If I were a little kid having this done, I think I'd be terrified. I felt we needed a safety word but then realized that if anything I would be the one zapping *his* machine and not the other way around.

"Okay, if you can hold still." As the tech wrapped wide strips of bright white tape around my head, it was clear I was going to be late for my presentation—even if I cabbed it back to the office. This was more important, I told myself as he finished up, my ears pressed flat against my head. The tape was so tight but not as tight as the imaginary metal band I'd felt tightening around my head at the end of every day for the past few months. Work had been a shit storm of constant changes and stress. The script for our latest young-adult project had originally been written in French, and the translation read so clumsily, it was laughable. The more I delicately explained to the producer that no credible American teenager would say, "I'm going to make the social media with you," the more she challenged my own grasp of native English. I laughed it off. The market testing would show how ridiculously off-kilter the dialogue sounded and we'd have to rewrite. It would cost more, but at least I'd raised the flag. After every one of these talks, I'd down a couple (or three) ibuprofen at my desk and tell myself it was just a tension headache, the kind that creeps from your shoulders up through the back of your neck and wraps itself over the top of your head like a malicious octopus. Everyone I worked with got them, didn't they?

"Now, if you can just lie back slowly and we'll get a baseline," the tech said as I caught a glimpse of myself in a video monitor. A hundred wires flowered forth from my head and I felt strangely glamorous for a moment in all my electro-brain-garb.

"Oh my God, how Bride-of-Frankenstein am *I*? Quick, we have to take a picture!" I reached for my phone in my purse, suddenly excited to be part of the whole grand experiment, and shoved it toward the tech. "I look like a total badass cyborg! My kids will love this!" I smiled cheerily as he snapped a photo, aghast. "Ooh, I should be singing like Madeline Kahn or that other chick from the original film! Elsa-something!"

I started to belt out "The hills are alive . . ." in a twittering vibrato. The bewildered tech took another photo and then quickly handed me back the phone. "Oh, come on." I winked at him. "I bet you never usually have this much fun doing these." He sighed impatiently and I lay back on the table. I knew I was a handful, but if I was going to be diagnosed with something serious I was at least going to be playing Maria.

You may wonder *how* it was or *why* it was that I didn't seem scared, but I *was* scared—that's exactly why I *was* singing. I was filling the air of that tiny room, which didn't seem big enough to house any truly bad news—never mind my bad singing.

As we went through a series of exercises involving flashing lights and some curious takes on Lamaze breathing, hyperventilating, and holding my breath, my brainwave Cy Twombly unfurled from the scratching machine.

The neurologist slipped into the cramped room. He was young, early thirties, and cocky with expertly mussed hair. It was clear he was a bright bulb, even if he was the *opposite* of a thoughtful, debonair Oliver Sacks-type I'd expected. I imagined him later in some hipster pickle bar, saying dumb, douchebaggy things like, "Hey bro, I know the three exact pressure points on your skull that will make you instantaneously crap your pants," in an attempt to impress other doctor-types.

He was quiet for a minute as he studied my Twombly, and I told him how the tech and I had just taken the best Bride of Frankenstein photo. He promptly ignored me and said, "Does anyone in your family have epilepsy?"

"Epilepsy? No." I dismissed the idea with one of those harrumph noises that people make when they're completely certain that you are an idiot.

I may have had a big seizure a few months ago and some ongoing weird symptoms, but that didn't mean I had epilepsy.

There'd never been any mention of anyone in my crazy lineage having anything like epilepsy, and if there had been, they would have complained about it nonstop and recommended all kinds of herbs. As far as I knew, my grandparents were healthy motherfuckers who lived well into their eighties and nineties. They said things like "I don't feel well, George" and then died quickly in rocking chairs. It was all very dignified. There was no rolling around on the ground, no thrashing, and certainly no public incontinence.

"Because *you* do." The neurologist's voice was thick with matter-of-fact medical orthodoxy.

"What?" I looked from the doctor to the tech, who now quickly excused himself.

"You've got the genetic signature," he said, now studying the patterns inscribed on the roll of printer paper.

In that moment, I felt all the air sucked out of that stupid, dinky room. My whole heart pounded off the walls. The malicious octopus was back. Its tentacles wrapped around my head, over my face, encircling my arms and legs. The idea seemed ludicrous, but good health had been my privilege—and privilege makes for blind spots, which can completely blindside you.

The only person I'd ever known with epilepsy was a dorky kid in high school chorus named Ryan. Kids were wary of the skinny kid in the baritone section. His seizures were severe and he'd always smelled a little like pee as a result. He'd had one in front of us once after practice, and I remembered breaking down in tears as a teacher swept in as Ryan's head hit the linoleum. I saw his eyes rolling back into his head, dark blood foaming out of his mouth from having bitten his tongue, and urine pooling beneath him. As his body shook, I'd never seen anyone so vulnerable. He looked like he was in so much pain. To me, Ryan's seizure had turned all his private adolescent humiliations into something terrifying and wildly public.

Epilepsy? No, it didn't make any sense. It was like I'd baked a fork into one of my pies. He had to be wrong. Wasn't epilepsy a childhood disorder? I'd never had a single symptom. Why now—at age forty? I knew I was juvenile in my general demeanor, but no one in my family had ever mentioned having anything even close to a neurological disorder.

And just because you have a big, starry seizure doesn't mean you have epilepsy. You could have a brain injury or a virus or a congenital malformation. Plus, wasn't epilepsy a chronic thing, where people had seizures over and over until their brains were so traumatized that they just died? I'd read WebMD. I'd watched the NFL. That wasn't me. Suddenly I was feeling the edges of a new emptiness, like trying to imagine drawing a box around the whole universe, but you just can't.

With sullen resignation, he said, "Chances are no one talked about it. There's a lot of stigma out there."

"So, I'm going to have more seizures?" All of a sudden, I was eight again. My voice shrank to that of a small child's. This couldn't be right.

"You will, and you need to be ready." He was making notes in my chart. I couldn't stand this guy.

"Wow, did you get like an 'F' in bedside manner class? Were you sick that day? Because I have to tell you, you are *no* Robin Williams." I could feel hot tears welling up. I am not a crier.

You may be thinking that this is the part where the handsome hipster neurologist empathetically places a hand over yours and says, "Don't you worry, you healthy, aspiring MILF, we're going to nail this. There are so many treatments compared to twenty years ago. We know so much more about the brain, and we've got a fucking dream team here that's ready to mobilize so that you can still have an amazing, badass life!"

Yeah, he didn't say any of that.

Instead, he handed me a wad of tissues and spoke a lot of words that cut in and out like a person with terrible mobile coverage. "It means we're going to try you out on AEDs . . .

antiepileptic drugs . . . and see what works. . . . Epilepsy covers a wide variety of different presentations. . . . You need to take the drugs consistently and indefinitely or you will seize. The first ones I'm prescribing may make you drowsy, but they are the least onerous. Also . . . going to order another MRI. . . . You may need to do a walking EEG if . . . blah, blah, blah . . . still having auras. Auras, being auditory or visual disturbances before the seizure's onset. . . . Sometimes, there's no warning."

As he continued man-splaining my brain to me, I remember how I'd felt like I'd died in that first seizure. The crawl back to being a functional, nonscary human being had been a complete Sisyphean slog. Now I was looking at a lifetime of multiple, repetitive deaths? Things were already uncertain enough as a single parent. And where I had been singing only a few moments ago, now I was being given a surreal death sentence of living through seizure after seizure that could strike at any moment. I couldn't put the kids through that kind of thing. Sophie already had a black belt in childhood drama. How many times can a brain spontaneously combust before progressive cognitive decline kicks in and I end up as a root vegetable? How am I not even dead from the last one? It killed me to think that I might be dying on repeat. And to do so over the course of thirty to forty more years just seemed the height of monotonous sadism.

I'd just been on a date with a not-entirely-horrible person—an actually plausible partner candidate. Now my new life partner was going to be epilepsy? Forget Jane Austen's Mr. Darcy. Forget Colin Firth. This guy "E" was going to be a really terrible, *bad* boyfriend, like Hugh Grant, one who showed up at all the wrong times when I was at my most vulnerable, only to push me in front of a subway train. And unless I was on medication indefinitely, he was going to keep coming back, again and again, to tell me we *belonged* together. In that moment, I could feel a cold knot twisting in my gut. Holy cats, I was going to have a seizure simply from *hearing* about seizures! What the hell was I going to do with all this electricity? And did this have anything to do with that goddamned fence?

"Ms. Jones? Are you listening?" Douche doctor was rattling off a litany of rules and cautionary measures all dealing with sleep, med consistency, stress, and baby-proofing.

I was caught in a riptide of either/or grim thoughts. When you're first diagnosed with anything chronic, you almost wish for the clarity of a terminal brain tumor. You're desperate for a finite amount of time and a knowable prognosis. With epilepsy, I could easily live into my eighties. It's like rehearsing for a play that might take forever to open. Thirty percent of epileptics lived with uncontrolled seizures, so meds might not even work on me. To be stuck so completely in the middle for decades? To be a burden to my family, or worse, my kids? *No way. I refuse*, I thought. I could feel my heels digging into the metaphorical dirt that is my own hardwired stubbornness. I have the will of Nietzsche and I wanted one option or the other—life *before* seizures or life *not at all*—anything but this uncertain electric purgatory. It was a kind of terrifying slippage, the ultimate in-between.

I was going to suffocate. The octopus was viselike now against my ribs and lungs. That's when the full panic set in. I started to pull at the tight tape still around my head. I had to get out of that coffin room. I had to get back to the office and present a stupid PowerPoint so that I wouldn't lose my job—not to mention my work-sponsored health insurance. This might be diagnosis day, but it couldn't be doomsday. Not yet.

8

The Cocktail Hour(s)

COME IN! COME IN! So glad you could make it! Yes, it's true. I've been hosting a literal party in my head for the past seven years. Just as there are many types of seizures, there are probably an even greater number of drugs, alternative treatments, procedures, devices, and diets now to keep the electric in check. I know some people liken their med trials to a cruel, long-term lab rat experiment, but overall mine have tended to follow a three-part flow similar to an old-school cocktail hour from five to seven in the evening. (Yes, I am trying to lighten the mood here.)

I realize this is somewhat of a ridiculous analogy given that most people with epilepsy are generally supposed to steer clear of alcohol, but indulge me for a quick second. Imagine you are at the end of a very long Thursday. You've had your share of fires to put out, various petty crises to avert at work, and so on. At five, you're sidling up to the dapper bartender in the dark, mahogany-paneled room and he's tempting you with various artisanal elixirs, but you're deciding between the sweet-bitter of a Manhattan with its whisky cherries and the cool, crisp tang of lime and quinine that is a gin and tonic. A few small sips into your cocktail and it's a now a lovely day. You start to decompress. You blossom into funny, charming, and chatty with just a spoonful of sugar to help the medicine go down. The deep relief of knowing you're not going to seize arrives in a kind of warm, watery, glowing euphoria, an expansive boundlessness like being a bit tipsy but never too much. At 6:00 p.m., your body and brain have started to acclimate to the cocktail. A snarky yet witty remark tumbles out of your mouth. As you reach a cruising altitude of confidence and calm with the meds you start to become yourself again, your *pre*-epilepsy *self*. You start to live your life almost like a normal person once more, but then there's a sharp turn. You have what's called a "breakthrough seizure" because, even though you're taking all the drugs, your body chemistry and particular triggers fail to prevent the seizure from happening. Maybe it's a minor seizure this time—a little jolt—more of a loss of time than a down-to-the-ground thrashing, rattling seismic event, but now at seven in the evening before you break down in tears, before angry vulnerability oozes from your every pore, you realize you need to get yourself to dinner *tout de suite*—toward the sustenance of a new approach and possibly a new med, different dosage, or add-on drug. And so, you start all over again with said cocktail hour. I became a regular at this, but it wasn't my first time trying to solve some riddle of myself. Plus, I was fortunate enough not to have meds stigmatized earlier in life.

It started with Joan. After all these years, I can still see the old girl standing half naked at the window before all of Manhattan, the Chrysler building glowing behind her like a beacon in a sea of skyscrapers.

"Please! Anyone who's interesting *at all* is on *something*," she proclaimed.

Joan possessed a glorious, grandiose Auntie Mame–like quality. Gliding through the penthouse wearing nothing but high heels, black pantyhose, and an industrial-strength slingshot bra that could have easily launched both casaba-melon-sized boobies to the moon and back, she topped things off with a giant, broad-brimmed hat awash in feathers. Why was she dressed like this, you ask? She always seemed to be in the middle of getting ready for something somewhere—a Broadway opening, the opera, or some secret, underground performance at La Mama. A film producer and hat company entrepreneur, she was my boss and mentor, and I truly adored her. Even when she corrected my California hippie grammar and podunk expressions. Example: "There's no word as 'anyways.' It's any*way*," she'd insist. Or, "It's different *from*, not different *than*."

I was in my early twenties, that crashing-around phase of life we all go through. I'd been whining about what I should do. Should I go to graduate school and be an absent-minded professor of film history? Grad school seemed like an excellent way of postponing any sort of real decision making. Should I try my hand at writing for film? Should I just see what happened?

I'd started seeing a shrink who wanted to put me on meds for anxiety and depression. I'd always been the neurotic sort, constantly debating with my inner Sylvia Plath in between periodic bouts of weepy incompetence. Still, I'd never thought of going the psychotropic route.

Didn't *most* thinking people relentlessly quibble with themselves? Wasn't agonizing over massive life choices part of what made them massive life choices? Wasn't it the drama in life that made us who we were supposed to be? Didn't the big, tough choices merit such conversations? Wasn't it an important part of being a full person? Maybe Joan had been right long ago.

Maybe meds would make the debates in my head more interesting and insightful.

But now with epilepsy, my pillbox looked like a doublewide trailer with the roof flying off in a twister. I was looking at a lifetime of measuring my days and hours in pills. I worried decades of meds would dull my senses and sedate me. Could people on these drugs even focus at work? What if I could no longer dream up pithy ad campaigns? How would we eat? Never mind the fact that I was looking at medication that had pronounced side effects that included deadly, necrotic, flesh-eating rashes, spells of intermittent rage, and insomnia—a common trigger of seizures. I tried to channel Joan in spare moments. How could this be interesting? How would this be helping?

Historically speaking, epilepsy remedies have been a rough ride for those afflicted. From the earliest recorded seizures by the Babylonians all the way through the mid-twentieth century, it seemed a "punishment-must-fit-the-crime" approach to scheming up new treatments. It's as if they all got together and said, "Okay, let's take one of the worst ailments a person can have and match it to the worst possible remedy, and let's see what we can get away with, agree?"

To get through these med trials and arrive at something that really worked would require a willingness to have things fail—to have seizures happen despite all the drugs, nausea, brain fog, weight loss, and side effects. And even if the "cure" itself didn't work for a while, I might witness some interesting happenings in my head, so maybe I should count myself lucky.

Humanity's most ancient form of surgical treatment, trepanation, was a grisly option for early fore-sufferers coping with epilepsy. As far back as seven thousand years ago, the practice of drilling holes into the skulls of patients was a common means of curing seizure disorders. Indeed, researchers often speculate that this gruesome form of brain surgery first came about as a tribal ritual and method for releasing evil spirits from the afflicted person's head. Archeological records suggest a fairly decent survival rate with many skulls showing signs of complete recovery, indicating that patients lived for years after the event—sometimes having the procedure performed a second time later in life and again surviving.

In ancient Greece (before Hippocrates) epilepsy, known then as the "sacred disease," was thought to be an illness resulting from an offense to the moon goddess, Selene. The afflicted would offer sacrifices, seek expiation, and take part in religious rites involving spending the night in her temple in an attempt to be cured.

Supporters of Hippocrates, the Greek father of medicine, believed that epilepsy had physiological origins rather than spiritual and attempted to treat the disease using humoral pathology: the theory that bodily fluids or humors were the primary drivers of health and wellness. The treatment was based on dietetics, or a structured, "sensible" lifestyle. This therapy was based on three pillars: dietary regulations, the regulation of excretions, and physiotherapy—so a moderate diet, keeping hydrated, and exercise. In addition to dietetics, early medicines, which were plant and mineral based and include copper, played a first, albeit minor role in controlling epileptic seizures.

In the Middle Ages, however, epilepsy was no longer considered to have physiological causes but was rather thought once more to be the work of devils, evil spirits, and demons ("morbus daemonicus"). As a result, therapeutic methods also reverted back to the spiritual realm of prayer, fasting, offering sacrifices, making pilgrimages, or undergoing exorcisms.

People turned to several saints for direct help or prayed to them to intercede with God on their behalf. Many sacred, devotional objects were used to combat epilepsy (treatment using the saints and sacred objects: "hagiotherapy"). After the plague, epilepsy was the disease with the most saints who were "responsible" for providing a cure, and the most important one in Germany was Valentin (probably because of the similarity of his name with the German words for "falling sickness," which is *fallsucht*, and "don't fall down," which actually sounds out as *fall net hin* or Valentin).

Beyond plain old exorcisms, the early clergy also held that epilepsy indicated the presence of highly contagious demons within the afflicted. Church leaders believed that if a person afflicted with epilepsy either breathed on or touched a healthy person, the demons would in fact spread to that healthy person in the same way as the flu or the bubonic plague. To prevent such airborne contamination, healthy people who had come in contact with epileptics were required to spit on them immediately, preferably in the eyes, which probably resulted in the poor person with epilepsy not only being completely grossed out but also now really getting properly sick with the latest cold virus—above and beyond already having seizures. Super. Just super.

Sixteenth-century doctors took a slightly more mystical approach and frequently prescribed extract of unicorn for the treatment of epilepsy, which of course doesn't exist. Native Americans and early settlers also used a tincture of what's known as False Unicorn, but in the end it was only found to be effective in treating worms and fevers. During this period there was hardly a plant that was not used to treat epilepsy. The most important plants were valerian, peony, mistletoe, mugwort, thorn apple, common henbane, belladonna, foxglove, bitter orange, and Peruvian bark.

Later in the Renaissance, chemical compounds also came into more widespread use for treating the "falling sickness." The most important of these were copper, zinc oxide, silver nitrate, bismuth, and tin. Other than sheer faith or perhaps the placebo effect, it's not entirely clear how or why these substances worked—if they actually did. Even to this day, it's not always apparent why one medication works and another does not. Where one patient has multiple AED medications fail without any concrete rhyme or reason, another's life is saved. It's a crap-shoot or a party, depending on how you look at it.

Beyond the Renaissance, the Victorians theorized that epilepsy was a side effect of too much masturbation arising from excessive libido and so recommended immediate castration for afflicted males. Mercury was also thought to help control seizures, but more often than not, the afflicted person died from straight-up poisoning before he or she ever succumbed to fits or other related injuries.

In one 1892 paper, a researcher claimed that excessive lust and debauchery frequently led to epileptic fits and that a person could self-trigger a seizure simply by eating large quantities of chocolate and listening to love songs. The condition was also dismissed as merely a punishment for morally lax behavior. For a time, Freud hypothesized that certain types of epilepsy were merely a form of hysteria or a personality disorder. This idea of an epileptic personality lent itself to a whole host of behavioral and moral prescriptions.

It was not until the second half of the nineteenth century, when people began to learn more about epilepsy and brain function, that drugs were finally identified that did have an effect on seizures. The first two substances that were proven to have an antiepileptic effect and that are still used today were bromine and phenobarbital. The side effects of the latter drug are that it's highly sedative, and this can get in the way of everyday function and quality of life. Today, however, there are more than twenty different substances that can be used to treat seizures, either in combination therapy or as a solo treatment.

Pharmacological advancements aside, the notion that seizures represent a kind of communion or coexistence with the spirit world or with the divine still continues to hold sway in a number of cultures today, so that different religious interventions persist in areas where treatment is less accessible. As late as 1975, Harvard neurologists Norman Geschwind and Stephen Waxman published research based on observations of patients coping with certain types of epilepsy during which they reported that many subjects displayed a high degree of emotionality, fixation on religion as well as a highly detailed thought stream, and an unstoppable propensity toward writing known as hypergraphia. This crockpot of behavioral traits posited that there might be such a thing as an epileptic personality. Over the next ten years, other psychologists appended hostility, aggression, lack of humor, and obsessiveness to the laundry list of characteristics supposedly associated with the condition.

By the mideighties, though, neurologists began to question the idea of the epileptic personality altogether. They pointed out that the supposed core characteristics did not appear in all individuals with epilepsy and that many also occurred in a variety of other conditions and disorders. By the start of the twenty-first century, researchers began to agree that only a select set of epilepsy patients exhibited some of these key traits and that curing the personality would not cure the disorder.

What are the neurochemical props of a contemporary life with epilepsy? I weighed the side effects against the disorder itself: necrotic, flesh-eating rash versus ongoing seizures. Which one was less likely to traumatize the kids or a partner? The most unsettling thing was that even my neurologist couldn't entirely explain how the drugs worked, and again, in one-third of cases, drugs didn't work at all, I was told.

There was no silver bullet. There would be no "Your Brain . . . solved!" slogan. That much was clear. My neurologist might as well have been money balling my medical fate in a basement in outer New Jersey. He was a curator of pills. But how would he even be able to identify the constantly changing psychological or physiological drivers behind the condition? "We'll have to check your levels." This would soon become a phrase I detested as it involved regular blood tests to ensure the drugs were present at standard therapeutic amounts known to stop seizures in humans. That said, you could be taking the highest dose and still experience auras or seizures, which, in my case, meant moving onto a new cocktail of drugs.

Trickier still, the various drugs affected different people differently. For one person, a certain drug might result in a miracle of being able to go a whole day without a fit; for another, a tragedy like seizing in front of a bus and dying. And often the very meds designed to save you proved problematic when used in combination. Or the side effects of one drug would leave you needing still other pills to counteract them.

One drug to control seizures might result in dark mood swings that then require an antidepressant that might, in turn, decimate your libido. So, then you need something for that.

This would then make your partner sad. He or she might need antidepressants thereby perpetuating the cycle of angst and anguish in your household.

Meanwhile, the drug to stop your seizures might also be doing a number on your liver. So then, not only is your partner not getting any nookie, now he or she has to donate a hunk of a vital organ as well. I keep waiting for the day when the doctor says to me, "Congratulations Ms. Jones! Your liver is now made of foam," and I have to borrow some liver from Ed or Holly. But it's all done in the desperate hope that one day you might feel well enough (or grateful enough) and want to finally *get it on* once more, which again puts you back at risk for still more seizures.

With the first AED trial came my initiation into the secret society of epilepsy drugs. Dilantin is an anticonvulsant barbiturate that works by slowing the brain's impulses. For me, it felt like walking around tipsy all day—as if I'd had a very strong Cosmo. It came with a creeping low-grade headache.

I didn't mind the floating feeling it gave me but found I could no longer walk in heels because it felt like I was always wearing two different heights of shoe: a kitten heel on one foot, a four-inch stiletto on the other. But actually, I was wearing flats. Yes, it was a small price to pay to be rid of seizures, but my balance was gone, which meant other things were gone too: like yoga and hiking. I'd be going about something as mundane as vacuuming the living room and find myself constantly casting around for a mooring in order to find my footing.

"You'll get used to it," my jerk neurologist assured me, but I didn't want to get used to feeling like I was living in an endless episode of *Absolutely Fabulous* (as much as I guffaw at that show). To live out my days as Edina seemed like a recipe for disaster, especially with kids in the mix. I certainly didn't want either of the girls to end up as grumpy as Saffron.

If I had to compare this drug experience to a Broadway musical, I'd say it was like *Wicked*. Everyone thinks they know the tale of *The Wizard of Oz*, but there was a whole lot more going on in that story than anyone realizes. One minute I'd be floating away in a bubble like Glinda the good witch and the next would find me completely green around the gills with Elphaba's pointy black hat tightening like a metal band around my head.

Worse still, I kept having auras—the visual and sensorial hallucinations that forewarned of a seizure. These auras were more of a thick brain fog. It was fraught with chronicity—that feeling of being dead while alive. This AED made reading words on a page next to impossible when I was having one, which was yet another impediment to earning a living.

The first AED was a fail. Going back to the pharmacological drawing board was a disappointing but fairly common occurrence the doctor told me. It would take some time and tweaking to get the cocktail right. I've heard other epileptics compare the process to feeling like a lab rat. For me, it was more like being a tourist in a very high-risk, low-reward travel immersion program. A year abroad nannying in the scary jungle that is your own head—complete with snakes, spiders, and other big bugs.

My next AED turned out to be the absinthe of epilepsy drugs for me. Serious road trip to beautiful-crazy-land. Suddenly, the very act of sleeping became an ultra-vivid Fellini movie. On the plus side, my vertigo and headaches stopped, but the cinematic sleep side effects could be downright overwhelming and frightening.

These dreams weren't like the luminescent fireworks of my seizures. They were so colorful they'd make a Crayola sixty-four pack blush. They materialized in full seventy millimeter with Dolby surround sound—all of which resolved into an overarching mood that was both surreal and fantastical. That said, the narratives were always spare and simple.

In one, I might be sunbathing on an island of craggy white rocks set against the glimmering Aegean Sea, surrounded by my closest childhood friends—key women in my life. We were all mermaids with underwater voices singing this strange aria amid the lapping waters. It was pure joy. No one could reach us. Still, we were safe. Some might say stranded, but we didn't mind it so much because there was this bright, very even feeling of reunion connecting us all, as if the sky were giving you a hug, brought so close you could feel its warm blue against your chest but without any sense of smothering or claustrophobia. Just calm, steady light. This dream was like a warm bath. I would wake from it in the early hours before the kids were up and yearn to be right back in it. It was a hunger pang, but without the despair of starvation.

Another dream found me standing on a life-sized chessboard with both my daughters starring as swaddled tots. Olivia was on a white square, and Sophie lay a short distance away on a black square near the edge against a deep crimson sky. All at once, the board tilted sharply to the left and we all began to slide and scramble. It was like a live-action version of Chutes and Ladders. As I slid on my chest to grab Olivia's hand, Sophie fell into the void. There I lay stretched across the board sobbing, and then it jerked again. Olivia was gone too. It was the mother of all nightmares—literally—as I'd lost them both.

My grief in this particular dream was so deep, I felt myself caving in and hollowing out. It was *dark*. And I was a black hole, my own fierce gravity turning inward and folding in on itself, accelerating at such a pace. I would wake up and do a big Michelle Williams–style ugly cry before the girls got up and think . . . this has got to be the drugs. And while I could take Fellini and the mermaids, I couldn't take the David Lynch chessboard of doom. It was too much.

That said, the meds were *technically* working. I'd stopped having daily auras and my seizures had become less frequent— down to once a month. However, when they did come, it was with little to no warning at all. I might be sitting with friends playing Bananagrams by the fire and suddenly I'd be gone. I'd be writhing on the floor only to awaken to one of them telling me everything was going to be all right.

Most of my seizures were less intense and shorter than on my first drug trial, so if I was home when I had one I could usually just go straight to bed for twenty to thirty hours and skip the expensive, exhausting drama of the ER. I never developed the flesh-eating rash that I'd been told could mean a deadly allergy to the drug, and my cognitive impairments were also not nearly as bad. I seemed to bounce back more quickly in the days following.

In talking with my doctor, it seemed that depending on random shifts in my metabolism, I could still burn through the meds and have a breakthrough seizure anytime, anywhere. In my case, I had the metabolism of a racehorse. My body burned through the drug like an addict. The doctor would increase my dosage, the dreams and an itchy (nonlethal) rash would come back, but then over the months, I would break through again with another seizure.

Beyond the guilt of feeling like a burden, the hardest part of this stretch of the med trials was the steady anxiety of walking around with the ghost of a seizure constantly whispering in my ear, "Hold up there, chica. Do you feel like you're going to spaz? Better get to a soft spot, pronto!" I needed to get better at anticipating them if this drug was going to work. I needed to be more realistic about what I could mentally and physically accomplish each day, to feel out my edges without always going over them.

My new boss was not happy. He was one of those managers who always walked around wearing food on his face. He'd grown a hipster pirate beard to hide his increasingly double chin—but his mustache kept morphing into an overly ambitious Tom Selleck toothbrush on his upper lip. He'd carp away. With each leveling up of meds, I was becoming less and less effective at work, which gave me a competency complex, making for even more stress and even later hours, which then made the meds less and less effective. Something had to give, but we'll get to that soon enough.

One thing that happens when you're diagnosed with a condition that's even remotely mysterious or chronic is that every alternative-complementary-holistic practitioner comes out of the woodwork with every possible remedy or cocktail of herbs to cure you. As I researched different options, it was clear that the wilds of the web were replete with blogs, think pieces, and social media postings by people who'd found their miracles in ketogenic diets, medical marijuana, or some shamanic ritual. All were cautiously cheery ("A Gluten-Free Treat for You!" or "Manage Seizures with Yelling Yoga!"). Most of the claims felt inconsistent at best, but they also reflected a deep unspoken grievance. Here was an entire population of people dealing with epilepsy, both wealthy and poor, some in developing nations and others in top-tier treatment programs, who were all linked by one thing: the inability of medical science to control their conditions.

I wish I could have more faith in the "fixes everything goop" that I'd been lured into buying on sites like Goop, but having worked on two reality TV shows in the recent past—both of which were about hopeless medical cases and attempts at alternative cures—I'd had most of my belief bled out of me by then. It was all trial and error. Nobody really knew anything, but still you *did* encounter a host of wild snake-oil-selling characters and personalities—a number of which were hilariously and sometimes tragically on an epic Holy Grail–style quest to solve some mysterious ailment of their own. But, per Joan, what doesn't hurt you makes you interesting and what doesn't kill you definitely makes you mouthy.

"You've never held a human brain in your hands," my doctor said, dismissing my concerns about how many seizures I was still having on my current meds.

"No, I'm holding one in my head and it's not working very well. Is there anything else out there? I'm worried my youngest child is going to have an aneurysm by the time she's twelve."

There was something else out there, but it would take some time and one very big misadventure to get it.

9

Why Yes, I Am a Cyborg

"GOOD GOD, talk about wearable tech," I thought as I studied my reflection in the overhead mirror.

Google Glass this was *not*. I looked like a gigantic walking tampon—a bright white Tampax super plus. My head looked too big and bulbous to be human. It was again covered in electrodes, which were held in place by thick strips of duct tape under my jaw. At the nape of my neck, a long ponytail of wires piped down into a tablet-sized data recorder strapped to my chest. I was an alien cyborg in poor disguise and I was on the bus. The lovely old silk scarf I'd used to cover things with wasn't quite doing the trick.

I pined for my analog wardrobe. I could feel the creepy-crawl of eyes on me now. This ambulatory or "walking" EEG was yet another test to understand my seizure potential triggers, and related nuances. The goal was to identify a more effective medication. It had been about eight months on this one AED, and I was still having tonic-clonic seizures about every month and auras all the time lately.

I tugged my scarf down over my headgear. When I was picking it out that morning, I felt I needed something from my old life *before* epilepsy. Some small thing to get me through the procedure emotionally. I'd gotten it on a family trip to the south of France five years before all of this upheaval, back when I was married and happy and couldn't imagine any other life than what I had—the kids, the meadow out behind our rambling farmhouse, and my funny, brilliant, handsome husband. Yes, on this grim, absurdly robotic day I'd wanted any part of *that* past to return. The scarf was a talisman to remind me that life could be good again. That it could be one of safety, stability, health, and a certain amount of permission to be as ridiculous and quirky as we liked as a family. Think: *The Royal Tenenbaums*, where every character completely owns their weirdness and claims it like a badge of honor.

I could have asked for a ride that morning, but I was supposed to be following my regular daily routine to see what sparked seizures and *this* was it. Taking the bus to work, being a goofball at the office, picking up kids from school, cooking over an open flame, and so on.

The EEG technician explained I would need to wear the contraption for three days without interruption. I'd had the option to do this exercise in the hospital, but that would mean missing work and finding a babysitter, which I couldn't afford. So, I decided to finally "out" myself—as it were—act like things were normal and just go into the office. The other moms dealing with cancer at school all had to brave the public eye in scarves and wigs. Why should I be any different? Yes, I might be a freak magnet in the short term, but it would be worth it if I could solve my seizures for the longer term. And if anyone would understand my cyborg cosplay it would be the video-game-writer nerds I was currently working with. If anything, they would want to participate in the experiment. The nerdiest among them might even find it hot. And no, the tech confirmed, I wouldn't be allowed to shower during the test, which these lovable dirtbags would most certainly understand as well.

My responsibility during the whole process: to keep an activity, aura, and seizure journal that I would then hand back into the doctor at the end for him to compare brainwaves with sensations and specific activities or events. Part of me worried about how specific my triggers might be. What if it was something I couldn't control? That would not be good. But what if it was something such as I could suddenly no longer have meetings with my new jerky boss? That would be awesome. On the other hand, what if it revealed things I didn't want to hear? "So sorry, Ms. Jones, we're afraid your favorite food (margaritas) causes spikes in electrical activity. Oh, and your free time, spent binge watching bad Canadian television while eating baba ghanoush with your fingertips—no more of that."

The data recorder itself made no discernible noises. As far as I could see, it was just a capture device; it wasn't like the beeping monitors you always see in movies. If I had a seizure while wearing my headgear, no sensor or alarm would go off—other than me falling to the ground and thrashing about, which, honestly, is alarming enough on its own. Still, I couldn't shake how self-conscious I was about the apparatus even if I *did* get one or two kind smiles on the bus with strangers working out in their inner monologs about what my story was. I'd decided ahead of time that if anyone, stranger or acquaintance, asked what was going on, I'd go full-on *operation plain speak* with them and say, "I have epilepsy. This gear is recording my brain activity to help prevent future seizures." With kids who asked, I'd keep things light and couch it as a cool robot experiment to better understand how brains work. If they asked what a seizure was, I'd tell them it was a lightning storm in the brain that was gorgeous to watch but also made me sleepy.

Thanks to smartphones, social media, working in advertising, video games, and teaching a science fiction film class in a past life, I already possessed a somewhat complicated relationship with technology. I had seen enough mad geniuses screwing themselves over with science, from *Frankenstein* to *Jurassic Park*, to have developed a rich wariness of a constantly vibrating, technologically determined life. Right now on the bus, I felt stranded smack-dab in the middle of the uncanny valley, that which makes us human and that which makes us artifice. This past year when Facebook's artificial intelligence robots shut down after they started talking to each other in their own language—one that no human could understand—people were appropriately creeped out. Likewise, my brain had started speaking in its own electrical language, which I was trying to figure out, but instead of people being freaked out, once they got over the initial shock of my ridiculous headgear, I noticed they were totally curious and overwhelmingly compassionate about things.

What makes us human after all? Self-awareness? Empathy? Will? Longing? Regret? Self-determination? I had always been mildly obsessed with how we come to know ourselves through technology. Now wearing my cyborg gear on the bus, I felt wildly self-conscious and even more human and vulnerable than ever before. The triggers of my seizures seemed rooted in the most basic of human activities: sleeping, breathing, seeing, and so on. I'd continued having auras on my current cocktail of meds. They manifested as a kind of buzzing lightheadedness. I'd talked to my neurologist about them and how I'd often feel on the very edge of a seizure while at work. I could always tell because I felt a kind of vertigo, always about to fall face first on the floor. Suddenly, I needed a walker with tennis balls on the feet or one of those *exersaucers* my kids used to hang out in right as they were learning how to walk.

There's no debating that we all live hyper-technologically mediated lives. What separates cyborgs from humans in so many science fiction stories is that people have will, appetite, desire, and a sense of purpose tempered with judgment. Cyborgs don't have that sentient wiring; they're not supposed to want or have an appetite for pleasure or pain. Having been raised to be somewhat of a pleaser, I definitely felt a certain pressure to act the part of a sick person and practice a kind of self-erasure or apology vibe to make people around me more comfortable. But if I did this, it actually might render the test results inaccurate. I also wasn't supposed to walk around like a Buddhist monk, all peace and tranquility. I was supposed to do my human, emotive, very stressed-out mom-act to better understand what triggers in that regular life were causing seizures and where they were located in my brain. I wasn't supposed to behave like a cyborg.

More interesting than how I navigated public space and social cues was how others did. Maybe it was the city, but being a fully wired robot girl had the opposite effect on those around me. I felt it most pointedly when I walked in to pick Sophie up from school. I'd assumed I would be a shock to all, and I'd steeled myself in advance to be gawked at by the other parents in class. There was only one other mom (that I knew of) who was visibly ill from cancer and wearing a similar headscarf. Yes, I looked a bit weirder than she did in that my head resembled the root end of a bunch of bok choy, but I was just another mother dealing with a health issue that sucks—so I needed to get over myself and suck it up.

I couldn't have been more wrong about people's reactions. Yes, there was the odd look or two on the street, but when I buzzed into the school to pick up my youngest, I ran straight into one of the dads I'd seen regularly at drop-off. He drove the same model as our old car. He and his wife had seemed very cool and smart at a glance—bookish and snarky and interesting. Both of them wore great nerd glasses. They seemed happy and like they cultivated the good kind of weirdness you want for your family instead of cultivating shoehorned blandness, which is what so many of the married moms appeared to be always striving for, and which I felt duty bound to resist given my unmarried, *Gilmore Girls*-ish status. I would never fit in with the traditional, married, minivan-driving, PTA clique of parents who had practical haircuts. I had already failed early on out of that particular demo by being divorced. In most schools, I'd noticed the wave of divorces didn't really happen until fifth or sixth grade. My kids had only been four and seven when my marriage ended and we were effectively on our own. From then on, it was always, "Did he cheat?" from the other mothers.

"No." I would answer.

"Did you cheat?"

"No. I totally loved my husband, our family, and the life I thought we were building."

Or, "You must have been a terrible bitch. . . . Are you crazy?"

"Probably. I struggled with depression and anxiety like a lot of moms do. WTF hormones? Plus, no sleep and career taking a backseat; it's a big adjustment."

And there was also, "What'd you do to go and lose a great guy like him?"

"I wish I knew. I would have done anything to fix things, but I wasn't smart enough or kind enough or ever enough. It haunts me to this day."

Still, these parents, whom I'd seen around school, seemed to reside in a world apart from the whole blame-oriented, judgmental parent clique I'd feared.

But now I stood there in the vestibule with this poor dad in shock at my overnight transformation and his first words were, "Whoa. You're Sophie's mom, right? What the hell happened? Are you okay? I'm Chase by the way, Ingrid's dad." He extended a hand.

He was wearing a green bowtie and a fedora and reminded me vaguely of the actor who plays Dr. Who, except more cool. I quickly explained my cyborg experiment for epilepsy and he immediately offered us a ride home. We lived about two miles from their house, but he said they didn't mind going out of the way. Flummoxed by the generosity and my daughter's pleas to spend a car ride with Chase and Charlotte's kids, I said sure.

Moments later, with Charlotte in the driver's seat and Chase quizzing the kids, and me in the backseat in a very animated conversation about everyone's respective days, I realized, "Oh, wow! This headgear of mine isn't a freak magnet, it's a *friend magnet*. I already freaking love these people!" Charlotte had Brigitte Bardot hair piled high, black sassy glasses, and a husky, former-smoker's voice. I had seen her all over school. In her past, premom life, she'd taught art history at the college level. Chase was some complicated type of consultant.

"Now, epilepsy is a type of brain spasm?" Charlotte asked.

"Err . . . sort of. My brain has too much electricity sometimes, and it all has to go somewhere, so, I have seizures. It's like a lightning storm in my head that manifests throughout my body."

"And you walking around wired up like a robot is just to figure out what causes them?"

I nodded. "Correct. It's a total *Frankenstein* cyborg experiment."

"That's amazing. So when they're done, you might know what not to do or they'll adjust your drugs?"

"I'm hoping. If it could be like a minor system-slash-drug update that would be completely great."

To my utter astonishment, these fellow parents (and kids) weren't weirded out at all by my situation. They were intelligent, funny, sophisticated, compassionate people who seemed to just get me.

I was so prepared for pity or shunning. For the first time since the first seizure, I wondered if upgrading your brain didn't make you less human but rather compelled others to be more so. Or would it be like most technology experiments? Would the potential upgrade come with new bugs and security breaches that need patching? Or would a small figurative code upgrade refine my judgment about people and the way I connected with people? Maybe I was making too much out of it, but I felt I understood for the first time since my seizures had started.

Work reactions were similar. Linda, the proverbial hall monitor from HR, complimented my scarf selection. I could tell she was probably a little worried about the visual distraction I posed, but she couldn't say a thing about it because epilepsy is a protected disability. The new boss didn't even notice, and while the nerds were trying to be respectful, their glee was abundantly clear as they inspected me as if I were a new toy robot. And it was also awesome *not* feeling like an imposter for once.

After three days, the main finding was lack of sleep led to unusual electrical activity from being worn down by the device itself because I couldn't sleep in the damn thing. Lack of sleep was actually causing me to feel "seizury," with a buzzing hiss in my head and the feeling of a metal band tightening at my temples. So, it essentially confirmed what I already knew. Nothing in my life was triggering my seizures other than lack of sleep, which I would work on getting more of, and there would be no changes to my meds other than to increase them slightly. It wasn't at all the outcome I'd expected, but looking back now, it was the best I could hope for because robot-me finally got to be human-me just a little bit more. And after all those months of keeping things a secret, I could finally be a spaz and have it be okay for the time being.

10

Dostoyevsky's Addiction

THE GALA INVITE READ "Love life. Hate epilepsy."
The cause was completely worthy—to fund advanced research to cure epilepsy, but the slogan didn't sit right with me. It felt like an alt-right extremist rally against the condition. I couldn't help thinking that I don't want to hate epilepsy. Hate is too exhausting. If anything, I want to get along with it so that it stopped being such a bastard. That was the whole point, wasn't it? Maybe I wasn't being hopeful *enough*.

Dostoyevsky loved his seizures.

Leave it to the Russians to make seizures into something fabulous, to elevate them to an art form and a cathartic experience. This is a country where potatoes become vodka, beets become borscht, and Siberia becomes a vacation destination.

Dostoyevsky's seizures always began with a bestial howl. There, in his drawing room, the writer would sit on the sofa talking with his sister-in-law. He might be in high, animated spirits chattering away when suddenly he'd go completely pale, lurch forward, and begin to fall. His wife would rush to his aid and notice a frightening change in his expression; suddenly there would be a fearful cry, a cry that had nothing human about it—and then he would fall into a grand mal seizure.

I'm probably not the first person to say this, but the epilepsy narrative can be very *dark*. There are *way* too many tales of woe. People need support for something so chronic, pervasive, and long term. Epilepsy is so much more than a seizure or fit. It steals moments, memories, whole childhoods, relationships, homes, job opportunities, and value from whole communities in that talented people find themselves housebound or unable to work or even stay out of the hospital. It's a shadow that follows without ceasing. It's the fear of being found out at work, of forgetting your medication, of becoming a shut-in. It's waking up to judgmental strangers. It's being written off as a drunk or a junkie. It's worried phone calls after midnight because you *didn't* check in, even though you are forty-three years old.

I thought of a woman I'd seen outside my office, wrapped in a foil blanket—the kind they give you in the ER when you're in shock or being rescued from Mount Everest. It had just started to snow and her cardboard sign said, "Just out of hospital. I have severe seizures. Please help. Very cold." She had shoes but no socks. She was in her early thirties and didn't appear homeless or like she was on drugs. Was this how her story ended?

From demonic possession to witchery to sexual deviancy— epilepsy brings some daring and destructive mythology with it. From being viewed as a genetic defective, someone who should never marry or have children, to being bullied, to horrifying stories of Nazis euthanizing or experimenting on epileptics during World War II, to stories of institutionalization in epileptic colonies, and to a beyond terrible narrative of a young woman being filmed by her partner while having a seizure during an intimate moment only to have the video end up on some awful website describing her seizure as a "literal death-gasm." There were too many narratives like these out there, online, where you didn't have someone like Dostoyevsky's wife rushing to catch him when he seized, to protect you from harm. A girl I'd come to know through one of my informal Spazzes-R-Us clubs had had a fit right as she was getting off the bus and people—in full view of the bus driver—moved her down the steps and just left her there on the street thrashing away.

Most of all, there seemed to be a whole tribe of lost souls, a vast archipelago of singular islands, each so conspicuously solitary as epilepsy varies so greatly from person to person. If you're anything like me, you *do try* in the face of a diagnosis like this to find any small nugget, some tiny glimmer of goodness or upside to it. Don't get me wrong; I'm the farthest thing from Pollyanna. I could win the crown for Miss Thanatos. Still, where was the upside? Where was the happy-ish medium? The comedy of errors that ended with everything back together? Or at least in a steadier rhythm? Where was the wisdom that supposedly comes from staring mortality in the face? Did it all have to be so repeatedly and profoundly bleak?

I don't know about you, but when faced with a crisis, I always look to history and my favorite role models for positive narrative outcomes. Most happy stories follow a common arc. Tragic stories have their own standard plot points as well, but most are not terribly original despite attempts to mix things up or flip the script.

I was so floored by my diagnosis that I became frantic for a different story. I would take any tale, any anecdote about how someone had cracked the code of their seizures with medication, surgery, or stories about who still managed to make a decent life after a diagnosis like this. Any story of "being okay" was a narrative to which I clung. Someone bearing witness to even one good thing before the potential descent into unyielding, biologically determined darkness was what I sought. I had to make it all mean something.

I needed a more hopeful narrative because if I accepted the idea that I had this random brain disorder that somehow no one in my family had bothered to mention was in our DNA, and that would never get any better, then suddenly my sense of self, my ability to make worthwhile decisions and to grow into even a slightly less idiotic person, felt out of my reach, and any control over life was illusory at best.

But when I gave my own pathetic, little sky-is-falling routine a momentary rest and looked at history, it seemed the club of known epileptics included an amazing class of creative thinkers, leaders, and even Olympians: from Da Vinci to Sir Isaac Newton, from Van Gogh to Michelangelo, from Harriet Tubman to Agatha Christie, from Emily Dickinson to Florence Griffith Joyner, from Lewis Carroll to Charles Dickens, and from Einstein to Prince. These were all people who would be amazing at the kind of nerdy dinner party I would so totally host.

The best of the bunch for me was Dostoyevsky who professed to fall in love with them, given the catharsis and creative exuberance he experienced leading up to them. Epileptic characters also feature prominently in his books and are believed to be based on his own experience. And while correlation is hardly causation, something in the narrative of these people made me believe that there was still a chance that life with epilepsy could be both highly creative and productive. In other words, I could let my seizures make life small or my brain's electric nature could be an opening to something greater.

According to Dostoyevsky, most of his seizures took place in the evenings, when he was either alone or with his wife. However, there are accounts of incidents that happened during the day, in the presence of other colleagues, friends, and family. These seizures usually began with what he called an "ecstatic aura." Auras can vary greatly across different people and sometimes involve music, sounds, odors, lights, visual disturbances, or other hallucinations. For Dostoyevsky, these auras almost always led to a loss of vision, language, memory, and consciousness.

Literary critic and the writer's friend Nikolay Strakhov related that Dostoyevsky often told him that before the onset of an attack there were minutes during which he felt unbridled ecstasy. Addiction is a disease, but what happens when you become addicted to the disease or the disorder itself? Not merely the high but the whole? Do you become a manifestation of addiction squared in a kind of vicious cycle? It's hard to fathom the idea of anyone being addicted to cancer or diabetes, but Dostoyevsky seemed to crave his seizures. He wrote feverishly around them. I recognized that craving, energy fascination with the altered state of the epileptic. What could my seizures teach me? Could I leverage the creative fervency around them to do different or better work?

Still, after Dostoyevsky's seizures, the world's foremost epic novelist would often lose his memory and in the days following he would describe himself as feeling completely torn down and wrecked. His mental condition was also despondent post-seizure: he could scarcely overcome his anguish and hypersensitivity. The nature of this anguish, in his own words, was that he felt he was some kind of criminal, that he was weighed upon by bottomless shame, by a fierce and wicked crime. I recognized this dread so palpably, so concretely, it terrified me. I've heard other epileptics talk about their self-loathing. This dread made me feel legitimately crazy and conflicted. How could anyone ever love me as a spaz? It made me want to live quietly, invisibly, and wisely—no late hours, no drinking, no stress, no excitement, and no heated emotions or passion that might start my fits. I would be a boring girl in order to avoid the repeated self-loathing. Wait, how was this me again? I'm not quiet. I am a loud, smart aleck-goofball-idiot.

What was also inspiring for me was how Dostoyevsky managed to make use of his auras and his seizures. Some of the most compelling characters in his novels are epileptic. Both Prince Myshkin in *The Idiot* and Smerdyakov in *The Brothers Karamazov* feel notably autobiographical and grounded in the writer's own experiences with the condition.

Prince Myshkin provides perhaps one of the richest literary characterizations of the seizure. Dostoyevsky also portrays how people with epilepsy are often viewed and treated by the culture at hand—isolated, freakish, and judged as less capable or intellectually disabled. In his depiction of Prince Myshkin, the writer also paints a striking picture of the emotional life of those who witness and respond to seizures. Prince Myshkin feels almost Christlike or saintly in that his emotions and intellectual capabilities are so compromised by his electrical episodes. Isolated from society by his condition, which is referred to as "the idiot's disease," the reader bears witness to the extreme stigma associated with the illness.

At the opening of the novel, the reader sees Prince Myshkin returning by train to Russia after a number of years in a Swiss hospital, where he was being treated for a peculiar malady of the nervous system—a type of epilepsy, with convulsive episodes. Prince Myshkin also shares with his fellow travelers that he hasn't ever learned a great deal from the Swiss experts about his disorder. I knew how he felt—for me it was the same.

In one passage, Dostoyevsky describes a rapturous sensation preceding one of Prince Myshkin's seizures:

> He was thinking, incidentally, that there was a moment or two in his epileptic condition almost before the fit itself (if it occurred in waking hours) when suddenly amid the sadness, spiritual darkness, and depression, his brain seemed to catch fire at brief moments. . . . His sensation of being alive and his awareness increased tenfold at those moments which flashed by like lightning. His mind and heart were flooded by a dazzling light. All his agitation, doubts, and worries seemed composed in a twinkling, culminating in a great calm, full of understanding . . . but these moments, these glimmerings were still but a premonition of that final second (never more than a second) with which the seizure itself began.

Dostoyevsky wrote *The Idiot* between 1867 and 1868, a time when he was experiencing significant financial and emotional stress. He had embarked for Western Europe with his wife, traveling amid various cities to seek treatment for his epilepsy and escape his debts. During his travels, the writer suffered an increased amount of grave seizures, which many around him believed were due to the stress of his poverty and fragile emotional condition.

In one his journals, Dostoyevsky recounted how he "was a long time unable to speak," usually a week, while another diary entry related that he still made numerous errors with the words when writing. These mentions of impaired speech, cognitive function, and sequencing following his seizures also felt hauntingly familiar.

What struck me most in reading these accounts was the bevy of intersectional factors in play—gender, class, education, neurology, heredity, biology, psychology, and politics. On the one hand, it sounded like another mirthless narrative to be disabled and dealing with chronic mental and physical illness that left Dostoyevsky cognitively impaired and suffering from extreme emotional highs and lows that came with his condition. On the other hand, while he sought out cures, endured hardship and destitution, and was even exiled to Siberia for his political beliefs, he still managed to salvage joy and inject deep meaning into his life. To empower characters like Prince Myshkin and to create the level of awareness of the condition felt profoundly heroic to me.

I was curious to understand how he also seemed to navigate cunningly the implication of moral failing that's so often associated with those individuals dealing with chronic physical and mental illnesses. Dostoyevsky's path seemed to carve itself through the act of *creating*, the act of storytelling, but without the theme of overindulgence attributed to epilepsy at the time. People tended to see the condition as a result of gluttony for experience: emotion, imagination, appetite, lust, and so forth, that set all the right conditions in play for a perfect storm to occur in one's brain without warning.

In the face of my diagnosis, I knew I would need to learn to navigate some degree of stigma, to trust in my comically broken brain, listen to its cues, and follow its lead. While my seizures seemed largely unprovoked—there were certain things that didn't seem to help matters: strobe lights, airplanes, too much time on all the different activities, and lack of sleep as indicated by my three days as a cyborg. And much as I dreaded seizures, I sometimes tempted fate. There's an allure to the velvety, black serenity of them. So, I'd get careless and stretch myself too thin across the various fronts of my life. It's the Enjoli conundrum. Bringing home the bacon meant staying up for two days straight that week working on a new commercial for my bosses. Frying it up in a pan meant baking a Tiffany-blue box cake, being snack-mom at soccer practice, organizing a sleepover for ten girls, and breaking things off with a grammatically challenged, not-so-significant other. Who *wouldn't* have a seizure? I woke up in the hospital with an intern standing over me, realizing I'd had a series of fits on a commuter shuttle in front of my entire work team.

At the beginning of an aura (which is something I experience rather than just see—it doesn't appear so much as it comes over me like weather), I often lose my breath. There's a moment where my heart goes quiet and a split second when my body senses that it's about to fall but my brain still hasn't yet agreed to it. The race to catch myself always feels like a sharp drag on a cigarette, everything shimmering at the edges as I force a slower rhythm to my breath.

I would also need to relearn how to trust my intuition about people, circumstances, and my own neurological limits. Women are especially conditioned *not* to do this. We're taught to interpret our instincts as anxiety or even hysteria. If we're caught listening to ourselves, there's punishment, judgment, and sometimes all-out exclusion. Indeed, my brain seems to have its own instincts about people, circumstances, and limits, and I often reduce those instincts to anxiety. It's my go-to response. I am a worrier—the quiet treasurer of the Scared and Paranoid Club. Sometimes your thoughts need a moment to catch up with your instincts. It's the moment when you know shit's about to go down, but you don't know what shit *exactly*. I used to do this with boys—the bad ones, the ones who are all wit, chemistry, and zero relationship longevity. They made my mind quicken and crackle; I was drawn to them, like a breathless, frenzied little moth, helpless to resist their flame—which was really more of a bug zapper.

My brain needs a grown-up to raise the volume of my super-ego in those moments. Another higher self or better version of me who will keep it safe from lightning bolts, necrotic flesh-eating rashes, and bad dudes. At the same time, my stern inner monologue needs to be tempered with some kindness.

As a woman, I can be a real asshole inside and out. When do you capitulate to the demands of typical female likability? How sick do you have to be? When do you need to be extra kind, even docile, speak in a higher, softer register because not only are you sick and therefore needy but also you're a chick and not an especially easy one to get along with? Are you beholden to a world that might let you stay alive if you kept the uncomfortable things about yourself safely under the radar, if you acted like a deep-cover spy, a sleeper agent in your own life? It certainly wouldn't be the first time someone tried to mask an illness in order to get by. But what do you do when history depicts your kind only as marginalized and sick? And no one wants to hear or talk about the condition because it's too much of a downer? What do you do when the routes to agency and subjectivity seem so bleakly inadequate?

Moreover, how do you write about epilepsy in a way that takes it seriously but doesn't succumb to grim plot points? Diagnosed, lost job, lost insurance, lost home, had more seizures, died. No, I was tired of afflicted female narratives, and I was also tired of the people who were tired of them. I know the "hurting woman" is a common trope in our culture, and I'm not keen on the idea that female suffering has gotten passé; it still really smarts. So, in writing about this very specific kind of pain, even with its extraordinary pyrotechnics, would I be representing a freeing of women's voices about chronic and mental illness or merely giving folks a small sliver of my experience?

I would be missing out on what felt like acres of time from my life, dealing with side effects, worrying friends and family with each ER stint, and enduring the inevitable crawl back to humanity every time a new medication failed or work put me over the top.

The black-eyed, bruised-body aftermath of each electrical storm my brain endured came with a loss of words, the inability to sequence tasks, the trauma it caused my youngest daughter, and the dread of how much it felt like I had died each time right in front of her. Hearing how she raced down the stairs to the neighbors' screaming for help. Pleading with friends *not* to call an ambulance every time I have a seizure. Never mind broken promises to bosses, insisting I had everything under control, ever-new excuses, pretexts, and outright fabrications about why I couldn't attend this or that function or event. Why I needed to go to bed early. Why I might again be late. Why I should or shouldn't be allowed to drive. My refusal to be solely defined by a genetic, chronic condition had left me defying it. Could I still thrive despite it?

Yes, my quirky, electric mind had made me who I am; I can forge connections across discipline, thinking laterally, to brainstorm a packet of fifty campaign ideas in an hour. I can read faster than anyone around me. I'm a chain reader, and my recall, my memory—while not photographic but more tonal eidetic or aural—is definitely strong when it comes to copy and content, words and images, and brands. I wouldn't have traded a seizure-free life to be an ordinary, linear thinker, but I didn't want the repeat injuries and drama. I just wanted my brain without the side effects.

The shame that accompanied each seizure also came with such an odd combination of euphoria and fatalism. If the lights could go out at any moment, why not just do whatever the hell I wanted and embrace my criminal side? I could make a really dark, *V for Vendetta* bucket list—full of fury and stealth revenge. I could work it like any system, any game of strategy, pattern, and recognition. It wasn't as much about playing the victim as it was about taking ownership of my particular brand of wiring, short circuits and all.

Yes, I'd been dealt a wild card, but I'd improvise and play it for all it was worth. So many others around me were also struggling with their own chronic conditions—everything from depression and anxiety to bipolar disorder and more physical manifestations like Parkinson's, Lupus, and MS—how were they flipping the script of their lives? While memoirist Jenny Lawson wasn't writing about epilepsy in her book *Furiously Happy*, I thought her approach of finding humor in the darkest of places—namely, crippling depression and anxiety—might work in my own narrative. She explores her lifelong battle with mental illness amid a series of hilarious essays that not only normalize her condition but also reposition it as its own special gift.

Lawson readily admits that many of her most favorite people are coping with serious issues, but you'd never guess that because they have adapted to dealing with it so authentically that to them it becomes their new normal. For her, being "furiously happy" was about "taking those moments when things are fine and making them amazing, because those moments are what make us who we are, and they're the same moments we take into battle with us when our brains declare war on our very existence. It's the difference between 'surviving life' and 'living life.'"

With my diagnosis, what if I took a dangerous, unpredictable, neurological liability and asked what if we adapted the world to this neuro-difference? What if we could find light in its darkness? Embrace everything that makes you who you are— the funny and the flawed or differently wired—and use it to find joy in unexpected ways?

It's hard for me to be prescriptive about epilepsy. First, I'm not qualified. Second, there are probably as many stars in the sky as there are people who want their seizures to stop, forever. But there may also be some who like their brains just the way they are. People who offer up a sense of humor, respect for their own differences, and an alternative voice that allows for myriad possibilities, plurality, and more hopeful outcomes, that is—to quote Temple Grandin—"Different . . . not less."

As Dostoyevsky demonstrated, a life with epilepsy (or with neurological differences, for that matter) doesn't *have* to be only about "surviving." It can also be lived with laughs, resiliency, and a powerful, self-determined narrative. If you tell funny stories about epilepsy, about being a spaz, and these stories do their job, readers may look up from the pages and find the "real" world of epilepsy, chronic illness, and neurodiversity more interesting, more human, more multifaceted, and more full of possibility.

11

When Mom Is a Werewolf

"A S FAR AS I KNOW I've never eaten anyone . . . yet," I told them.

I'd had another grand mal while walking into our kitchen. Sophie told me I'd fallen backward this time, and I could feel the knot growing behind my left ear. I had no memory of this one, but my tongue was swollen where I'd bitten it and was bumpy as a cauliflower.

Etched indelibly on the film of my 1980s adolescent memory was the scene from one of my favorite films *American Werewolf in London*, where the actor David Naughton (also of Dr. Pepper fame) wakes up totally naked in the park next to a bloody deer carcass. I'd felt like that all the time since my seizures had begun. Always caught out. Without even knowing it, my brain had made me into a disobedient, unreliable shapeshifter, except I wasn't even governed by moon cycles. Indeed, there are whole chunks of my life—minutes, hours, even days—where I have no idea what I've done because of this. It's a werewolf-ish feeling and accompanied by much postseizure dread and pending regret. It's that waking phase where I'm vaguely aware that much may have gone down while I was out, and I don't know—and I don't know if I want to know it. Yet.

It's that cringing feeling of, I did *what*? I said *what*? How can you regret or apologize for what you cannot remember? Perhaps the same way I had apologized in advance to my kids for all the things that might go wrong in their lives? This felt different, though, because things *were* actually still going very wrong. While we might have to improvise on the fly at times— meaning a neighbor might have to catch me midfall, or my daughters might need to recount my medical particulars to a stranger or cue me to get to a safe, soft place before a fit—I felt we needed to confront the beast head on. We needed a vivid, funny, and memorable action plan, an overarching, relatable metaphor to contain it all, with code words and protocols, one that satirized as much as it empathized, one that made seizures less scary and reminded everyone that I was still me.

I've never been fully present for my seizures, which is fairly common with the condition. Again, there's the sense of ecstatic peace I feel right before I go into one, the visual fireworks, leading to darkest dark, and then profound disorientation, fear, and confusion upon waking up. I tend to never have any solid memory of the actual on-the-ground thrashing bit. For all I know, I could have marched politely over to the neighbors' yard and tried to drink the liquid out of their hummingbird feeder. I have no idea about anything I might have said or done. It's just a black break in the footage of my memory. Even when I try to slow the tape, there's nothing there.

In a fashion akin to Miss Marple, I tend to gently quiz people after they've been through a fit with me. I've become used to imagining a version of myself flailing around on the floor, eyes rolled back into my head and crying out as though there is an angry wasp trapped in my throat—all while still being moderately alluring. Charlotte would say, "You always look like you're having an amazing orgasm when you're seizing. Your hair looks so good afterward." Indeed, the "howl" transformation to full fit has been described to me as a cross between that wide-mouthed clicking sound the scary girl from *The Grudge* makes and a mime doing a "walking-down-stairs" bit behind a sofa where you just go lower and lower with each step because your legs have morphed into overcooked noodles. I usually fall backward when I seize while walking and apparently it looks pretty silly and scary.

There's actually a real benefit to this method of falling backward because over time, with repeat hits to the same part of the scalp, you get only a bald spot on the back of your head instead of say falling forward and breaking your teeth. A bald spot can be covered ever so much less expensively than loads of trips to the dentist. And I'd planned for kick-ass colorful wigs if I ever got to the bald stage. It was either that or glamorous clip-in extensions.

In any case, even on meds, apparently I still do a fair bit of crashing around when I'm at peak spaz, and it had become clear that our household needed a set of instructions to bring me back to human, to decrease the anxiety and help people feel like seasoned professionals around me during a fit. I decided they needed to be werewolf experts.

Some people might take offense to animal metaphors or my likening epilepsy to lycanthropy, but when I was searching for an analogy, I needed pop culture on my side. Having a seizure does not make a person a monster, but it is a very *definite* experience for those around you. The werewolf-cum-creature of the night concept was simply one way of framing it that worked for our household. We'd just endured the whole *Twilight* saga, so it felt familiar and slightly more empowered and badass than other comparisons. Plus, historically speaking, there were clear rules and protocols to follow when it came to werewolves. We needed those cue cards front and center to diffuse the fear. So, multiple, laminated copies of the seizure to-do list and script for when Mom has a fit became the big project. The point was we needed something semipermanent and codified that would guide people around each event, especially since the werewolf can't speak for itself during the moment, which is almost always the case with me.

Now, according to werewolf lore found nearly everywhere on the Internet and in medieval Eastern Europe, there are three approved methods for curing a victim of werewolf-ism: Medicinally, usually via the use of wolfsbane, which sounds like a fun herb to try, right? Just kidding, *do not try this* because I don't even really know what it is; I'm a New Yorker, not a botanist. Surgery—also very scary. Or exorcism, which could easily count as me writing this book. Aside from the obvious parallels one might draw with epilepsy treatments throughout history, there were other werewolf best practices that I thought might hold some value for our seizure emergency plan while making it easy to remember at a moment's notice:

1. *Love that fenced-in area.* Turn me on my side, clear any hazardous objects immediately surrounding me, but don't actively restrain me. This is a deal breaker as people who have seizures may exhibit absurd strength during a fit, and it's possible for you to get hurt or for the person seizing to hurt herself. Turning the person on her side also helps to prevent

choking due to foaming at the mouth or heaving one's guts out. Wee. Good times.

2. *Watch the fangs.* Never put anything in the mouth of a person who is having a seizure. I promise I won't swallow my tongue. I might bite it, which is why you sometimes see blood foaming out of a seizing person's mouth. And while you want to be sure the person is still breathing, no one wants to lose a finger.

3. *Embrace the faux-fur, people.* Grab the nearest soft thing to protect the person's head, face, and teeth. If out in public, a coat folded up under the person's head works great. In our house, stuffed animals or fluffy couch cushions with washable covers have been the go-to. We also got a super-girly faux-fur rug for the living room that works well. The best invention I've ever heard of came by way of our neighbor Zach. It was a motion-sensing inflatable airbag helmet/collar originally invented for cyclists that you could wear around your neck. If it sensed you were about to fall in any direction, it would automatically inflate to protect your head and neck from breaking. Yes, such a thing actually exists. And given the state of my forty-something-year-old neck, this seemed like something to try, especially if I could accessorize it with glitter, a scarf, or a statement necklace.

4. *Even werewolves take a while to transform.* So, always time the seizure. If ever you needed an excuse for a new smart watch, having a spaz for a friend or family member is an awesome one. Until they really *do* invent a Fitbit for the brain, timing a seizure is important for EMTs and doctors to know what to do next. If the seizure has gone on for more than five minutes, or if there are life-threatening injuries, breathing issues,

severe lacerations, or a concussion, our household proto-col is to call 911, preferably with an adult on hand. If it's a shorter seizure, I always liked to recover at home in my own bed, with my family and amid familiar surroundings—so I had a note that declined transport that could be used. The ambulance alone can run thousands of dollars in some cities, and I've always found the hospital to be the least restful place on the planet. Between the medical device beeping and chaos of other ER dramas unfolding, it does me in every time. Ambulances are also a problem in certain cities as landlords can evict a person if the emergency services team comes more than eight times to a single address. It's absurd and cruel to think about losing your house or apartment because your family called 911 to save your life, but this is why we need so much more research, accommodation, and advocacy for people with neuro-differences.

5. *Remind me who I am and who you are.* You know how in every movie about werewolves, there's always the scene between the wolf and his/her friend where it comes down to a moment when the friend is all "It's me! You *know* me were-wolf Alisa! We're besties—not beasties! I know you're still in there somewhere. Please, don't eat me!" It's the same with someone having a seizure. Chances are when I'm waking up from one I'll be frightened, be disoriented, and have zero memory of what's just happened. I may not understand where I am, who I am, or who you are. In fact, I may look at you like *you* are the monster and be terrified. Remind people seizing that they are safe, who they are, who you are, that you've got them, and that everything is going to be okay. To keep talking calmly to the person is, I believe, the best pos-sible thing you can do in the moment.

But what if you're home alone? It may sound extreme, but I read about a woman who lived alone with severe epilepsy, and she actually spray-painted instructions all over the walls inside her house to remind herself of her full name, that she was home safe, and that she was loved so that when she woke up from every seizure, she could ward off the inimitable terror of having no memory. Her landlord must have been a saint. Still, the most important thing if you're ever having a seizure while alone is the ability to self-identify and recognize your immediate surroundings. Your recovery from the moment begins there.

If you've ever had a really bad hangover, just multiply it by a thousand-kajillion-million and add some miscellaneous injuries, deep shame, and despair and you'll have an inkling of what you might feel like after a seizure. Hearing a caring, steady chant upon waking, one that reminds me that I'm still *me* (and not a wolf) and that everything is going to be okay makes such a difference every time.

6. *Keep an eye on the moon cycles.* I know it may sound all Stevie Nicks and Wiccan (not that there's anything wrong with that; witches are cool), but I mean this to simply say keep an eye on your own internal systems. If I know I'm going to have a seizure or if I sense one is on the horizon, I can sometimes prepare in advance not to terrify, embarrass, or injure myself. As I've mentioned, for me an aura can be anything from a shimmer to an electric current sensation to the feeling of a metal band tightening around my head, and in some cases, I can't tell if I'm moving forward or backward and so I feel both at once. It's more psychedelic than painful.

Admittedly, I do need to come up with a better code word for it to help alert people around me, but these days I usually tell people, "Sorry, I've got to 'werewolf' myself, people." The upshot is that I typically leave work early with the help of a friend, I go to bed with the requisite number of pillows (five or six), and I take some powerful emergency meds that I keep on hand that can help to ward off the onset of a seizure. This foresight, however disruptive to daily life, is the best way I can get myself to a safe place before things go down and reduce the drama for the people around me.

I read about a man who had very short auras before sudden severe seizures. His mode of dealing was to lie down wherever he might be and bite down on the wallet that he always carried with him. He did this to protect his tongue before his seizures would start. I've been on the lookout for something to bite down on for a while because I do not want to use my wallet. As I mentioned earlier, it's attached to a big bag that I really, really like it and so that's one thing I categorically will not sacrifice to epilepsy.

7. *Remember: technically, the werewolf is only on the hook for manslaughter, not murder.* What this means is that in terms of the odd things you might say during a seizure, other spaz friends of mine have said extraordinary things before, during, and after their grand mals. One friend who was regaining consciousness after having a seizure on the trading floor of the investment bank where she worked told me she could not stop screaming, "Don't take me to jail!" as the paramedics carted her away on a gurney past shocked finance bros in suits. Oh, how they must have been shitting bricks. It may have been based on what she'd seen with other colleagues,

but she was absolutely convinced in the moment that she was headed for the clink. All this is to say, reserve judgment, you good Samaritans out there. Confusion, disorientation, and straight-up terror are common after a seizure.

I've been told I'm pretty funny coming out of an episode. Apparently, sometimes I know things I *never* thought I knew, like obscure phone numbers. There have been other times in the aftermath of a seizure where I've thought, Holy hell! What do I really know that I didn't know I knew? Maybe I know karate? Or Portuguese? Doesn't that language have more than seven thousand irregular verbs? In this regard, my seizures somehow feel less regrettable. And there's a hope for better moves with martial arts for sure.

8. *A reminder for the werewolf minders.* It's important for the people helping the person having the seizure to take a breather. I generally sleep for two to three days after one—not everyone takes this long to recover. I think it may be that I use so many muscles in my body during each episode—plus, there may also be injuries. For the people helping me, it can be traumatic, seeing the transformation the person goes through from aura to seizure and to the postictal recovery. Seeing a loved one so profoundly helpless, vulnerable, and possibly hurt can make for major anxiety, depression, and PTSD. It's okay to take a break. You need to look after yourself in whatever form that best takes.

For the person having or who's had a seizure, it's okay to be bummed if an ambulance was called during the event. Hopefully, they administered oxygen and gave you decent meds. Yes, it can lead to unanticipated medical bills, the loss of a driver's license (probably appropriate even if totally inconvenient), and all kinds of other daily life consequences, but *know* that the people around you were probably doing the very best they could to keep you safe. Thank them. (Thank them with pie!)

To the wolf minder, it takes a while to process *experiencing* a seizure on all sides, which is why giving you and your wolf some room to roam and breathe is key—all the while remembering that you are pack animals together and having each other's backs is key to improving quality of life and reducing fear around each event.

12

Everything in New York
Is a Little Bit Broken
(Part 2)

Looping back to "the big one" in 2015, Delia-the-neurologist—like my girlfriend Holly—was a feisty woman. I vaguely remember the argument between Walter (the head of the hospital's maxillofacial surgery program) and Delia. She was so small next to him. Her head only came up to his chest, but she was fearless and fierce. She was wagging her finger in his face and they were going at it. I couldn't make out exactly what they were saying as their voices had morphed back into Charlie Brown *mwaw–mwaw*, but it was something about seizing on the operating table, how I would die or be terribly maimed and/or probably scare the poor band of impressionable surgical residents out of medicine altogether. They reminded me of two parents arguing over what to do with a troubled child. I felt the heat of their tempers flare, and I thought I saw them both glow orange in the haze of my room. That's when they took it outside and came to a compromise. I wasn't frightened or sad at this point.

I think I was more just relieved that they'd found me and that they were working things out. Meanwhile, I faded back to black.

The surgery would go forward the next day at dawn. Making an incision up the right side of my face from the crown of my head down to my chin, they would peel my face off from my skull with the goal of rebuilding what was left of my lower jaw with pins and plates and then reattaching both sides to my upper jaw and head with rods, making any alignment adjustments arthroscopically, sewing up the fracture lacerations, and wiring me shut—all without severing my facial nerves—so that I might still be able to feel, taste, blink, and smile one day. My front teeth were gone, but my tongue was still in one piece. Teeth could come later. It's so strange now to think of myself as having been in so many pieces, like shattered china, but there I was.

A S I WAS BEING WHEELED into the operating room, Walter's own jowly wizard face gave me confidence. I thought if anyone could put me back together, it would be this mad genius. With whatever drugs I was on, he looked just like the professor from *Back to the Future*. I fixed my thoughts on my daughters— just to hold them in my mind's eye for a second longer. They still had no idea about the extent of my injuries. In my head, I thought I heard David Byrne singing, "This is not my beautiful life . . ." but I think now it was just Walter humming. He hums when he works, I would come to find out over the next eighteen months and three more surgeries.

I thought back way to the last kiss I'd had with the man I'd been seeing, Pepé Le Pew. The person I *didn't* want seeing me now, at least not until *I* had seen me *first*, but I was homesick for him. For that kiss, the scent and friction of his scruff. Did you know the second most-asked question on the Internet is how to kiss? Some writer somewhere must be quipping that the real question should be *how to kiss like you mean it*. I could feel that kiss, that future life receding from me now, folding in on itself like a dead star. You were too happy, said the cynic in me. That's why this was happening. I don't know how I got the words out before going under, but I asked Walter, "Do you think I'll ever be able be to kiss again?"

And he didn't sugarcoat or make false promises. He simply said, "I don't know, kid. Everything in there is a little bit broken."

I WASN'T GOING TO be able to *Life Is Beautiful* my way out of this one.

As the blurry forms of Holly's face resolved into focus, I could just make out her halo of strawberry-blonde hair. Her smile lines formed parentheses around her straight, white teeth. (Sigh . . . teeth!) Her little black glasses lay perched low on the bridge of her nose. I went to speak, just to ask how things went with the surgery, only to find myself seemingly sewn shut. Frantic, I searched the inside of my mouth with my tongue and felt the inner jagged remains of my front teeth, a crooked graveyard of tooth shards, but there was no opening for my tongue to slip through, no way to part my teeth or my lips, open my mouth, or make sound. I felt myself inhale sharply, loudly huffing through delicate nose hairs. There was no opening for words. I started to panic.

Inside my face and head everything felt oddly splintered. Like tiny tent poles, a dozen or more pins held the skin of my cheeks and chin away from my skull and face bones. The sound of my breathing echoed inside against my inner cheeks. I was like a huffing rhinoceros or a jowly Richard Nixon—take your pick.

Holly leaned forward, sensing my anxiety, and spoke in hushed tones: "You're going to be okay. The surgery went well. You're okay. Just breathe through your nose. They had to wire you shut. Your jaw was in a spasm and pulling hard to the left. That's right. Breathe, *chica.*"

I remembered, I remembered. I would need to be wired shut to heal, they'd told me. Everything was a little bit broken, so no talking. No solid food, only liquids. Good God, what was that smell? Everywhere around me now was the odor of briny, salty seawater, but with something extra. As a mother, I immediately recognized it. I'd inhaled the biting stench of a soaked dirty diaper. Holy crapdazzle, it was me! I had the worst morning breath in all the world. It smelled like I'd licked the subway and then let it fester in the New York City heat amid some raw sewage. These were not similes I could deal with at this time. I gestured to Holly for my pen and paper and slowly wrote, "Got a mint?" out in big block letters. Even wired shut, I figured I could at least fit that in between my cheek and gum. She laughed, "Let's see if we can get you some mouthwash, lovie" and went to track down the nurse.

I ran my fingers lightly over the puffy planes and new angles of my face. I willed myself not to panic as I felt the metal staples just under what had been my hairline. What I'd seen with epilepsy thus far was that the body could shift and change very quickly, so no crying yet. The pins in my midface area just under the skin of my cheeks felt like tiny dollhouse doorknobs. I didn't seem to have significant stitching on my face, which was a relief. I gazed around my room. There were paper signs stuck up on the wall above and beside my bed: FALL RISK, SEIZURE RISK, BROKEN JAW/FACE—all in urgent, black Sharpie. That must have been Ed's doing. He loves signs. The nurses seemed a tad frightened of me, but having seen my mummified selfies, I would probably be frightened too at this point. Epilepsy now had me squarely by the lady balls.

The nurse came in with mouthwash and to explain the glorious clicker of pain management. A morphine drip with a remote control. Anytime the pain started to flare up, I could hit the clicker to make it go away. I hit the clicker three times to try it out. As I felt the opioid goodness flooding my system all the way to my neon-yellow gripper socks, I thought, *It takes a lot for me to blow out my hair, but I would so totally go out on a date with this robot-machine-thing. I could use one of these, but for my whole philosophical-emotional life, an existential pain-management clicker.* I hit it again. No wonder people liked drugs so much. This was like chasing Xanax with really good weed, chased with . . . chloroform. It was fantastic, even if I was Tutankhamun. (Know that I'm not making light of America's addiction to opioids, which is very serious; I'm just saying I relate.)

Holly returned with one of the young hot residents—Dr. Some-Italian-sounding-delicious-truffle-name—who checked my cranial staples. (Cut me some slack, I'd clicked three times. I was home.) He had such *great* skin. And his hair! It was *ER*-era George Clooney hair—clean, yet scruffily mussed, but there was no man bun on this millennial. I think if I could have smiled, I would have, but I couldn't move my face or much of anything at that point. However, when he left, apparently I grabbed Holly by her Prada tunic and tried to get out the words, "Holy hell, did you see that guy?" Except she said it came out sounding super loopy, so it took her a while to decipher, but she nevertheless concurred. But how could I break my whole face and still be so insistently shameless? What other things had I said or done? And *when* was everything going to be a little *less* broken?

13

Unspeakable

"**V**UCK OFF, MARILYN. This *is* my yoga," I told her. I love living in a city where the F-word is mandatory—even when I can't say it.

I'd been singing again for my speech therapy—even though I still felt wired shut. My nine-hundred-year-old neighbor Marilyn stood in the doorway preening her dust mop of a dog, Biscuit. I love pooches, but that poor animal always sounded like it was being kicked in the teeth, which did not bode well for my current facial/dental PTSD. She adored the little guy—so there was nothing to call the mayor about. Still, I felt zero guilt about being noisy or dropping the odd F-bomb or two. What can I say? Even in my wiser middle age, the inner tough-guy street rat that sometimes commandeers my frontal lobe is still convinced that swearing makes you stronger.

On the other hand, there *are* circumstances where all it does is terrify and trigger people. Right now, I needed to terrify and trigger Marilyn to go away. She was giving me *what-fer*, as Ed would say.

Marilyn was the kind of person who could always be heard whispering in the street to her dog, "No, you don't always get a

cookie for doing the right thing. That's part of being an *adult*."
Something loud and insane was always afoot on the other side
of the wall at Marilyn's: illegal construction, intense granny
raves, the odd kidney transplant—something that always made
the dust mop crazy with yipping. You never quite knew.

"Marilyn, I had to buy sniper headphones when you and
Biscuit moved in, so you can't talk to me about noise."

"You know, your speech is getting much better."

It's true. It was. I'd been singing "The Way You Look Tonight."
Before that I'd attempted to belt out Fiona Apple's "Criminal."
I am not an especially good belter, but Fiona's lyrics seemed
entirely appropriate given the police state of the city that day.
The terror threat level was at chartreuse.

Still, at this point, it was all about getting language back and I
didn't care if Marilyn, her dog, or the terrorists heard me. In the
hospital, on pain meds, I had hallucinated all kinds of gleeful things
my teenaged daughters might say now that I was wired shut:

"Oh my God, she can't talk. *This* is the *best*! She can't nag me
to wake up in the mornings anymore," Sophie would say.

To which Olivia would reply, "She can't tell me to clean up
my crafts or complain about all the glitter!"

Then Sophie's eyes would widen and she would gasp, "She
can never embarrass me at school functions ever again!"

Only to have Olivia knowingly chirp, "Oh, she'll find a way."

"I really hope she stops wearing those stupid tank tops that
say things like 'Organic' with a bean sprout and 'Reading Is
Sexy.' Ooh! Do you think she'll just stop talking altogether?"
Sophie wished out loud.

With Olivia expressing her skepticism, "Hmmm . . . I don't
think she can. Not without going even more bonkers than she
already is."

At one point, even our old nanny made an appearance and said something along the lines of, "*Aye, Dios mio*, it's a miracle, Miss Olivia! God has answered our prayers!"

In the middle of all this, coming to grips with not talking, I tried my hand at sign language and learned how to say things like, "I can hear you. I broke my face and so it's really painful to talk."

I have to confess; there was something wildly satisfying about communicating this way. I was crazily frustrated inside my head and mostly expressionless face, so to be able to use my hands to emote felt great. A number of the signs are highly intuitive and vivid so they're completely easy to learn. The sign for the word *painful* is two hands twisting knives into your ribs and the expression of agony. The problem was not enough people around me knew sign language to comprehend all but the most hyperbolic of charades. There was a period after coming home where I was always on the lookout for the signifiers of deaf culture, say on the subway. I would search for anyone who might understand me. With hearing aids getting smaller and smaller, not to mention miraculous cochlear implants, it was hard to tell who might be a fellow understanderer of ASL.

Technology would be my answer for the near term, I thought, testing out a finger sketching-spelling app on my iPad. Of course, it's still clunky as hell if you have terrible finger penmanship, which I did after all the drugs. Plus, I could see that people always felt they had suddenly been put on the spot and were being challenged to an impromptu game of Pictionary. Overall, the moms were the best at reading my looping iPad scrawled messages, but the net result was that my impatience to speak, coupled with their impatience to understand and correctly guess my words, just made for more impatience.

I knew there were a number of iPad type-to-talk applications out there on the market. This was my next stop in moving toward communication. I downloaded several to figure out which was the most "human" feeling. I knew I had a great deal of communicating that I would need to do when applying for my upcoming disability claim. I also felt I needed to choose a voice that didn't sound like every car GPS or every virtual assistant out there. It needed to sound a little like me. I wanted a woman who was not too robotic, so no Siri, no Alexa, and I didn't want her to sound too posh. I wanted someone in the vein of a friendly British newscaster, and I was elated when I finally found her. She sounded just slightly less aristocratic than the BBC World Service's Sue Montgomery. I practiced typing out common phrases in the app to have them at the ready for public interactions. They were ordinary things like "please" and "thank you" and "Can you help me?" or "I'd like to order the ——" or "I'm so sorry. I was in an accident and so I use assistive technology to speak."

I remember going to the disability office in Harlem and being so proud of myself as I pulled out my iPad to engage a giant prison-guard-looking-guy behind the desk to ask for help. I pressed play on my iPad after typing in my question and Sue Montgomery-me spoke politely to the guard. His face screwed up as he listened. "What's it saying? I can't understand . . ." He was shaking his head now.

I hit replay and Sue Montgomery-me repeated the question, which I think was something absurdly basic like "Hi, I'm trying to find the disability department. Can you tell me which floor it's on?"

"Look lady, I don't know what this is. Can you hear me?" He started talking really loudly now. I nodded yes and flashed my teeth to show my wiring. I also played Sue again, saying, "I can hear you. No need to shout. I just can't speak."

"Lord, if I ain't seen it all," he sighed, handing me a clipboard and a pen. I wrote out my question in my crap penmanship, which he ultimately understood. So much for technology. It was also clear that even at the disability offices (at least this one), the staffers weren't necessarily used to applicants trying in earnest to adapt to new modes of communicating. I was back to pen and paper for most interactions.

I DON'T KNOW WHAT I WAS expecting four weeks later when they finally fully unwired my mug. For those first terrifying moments, I thought my lower jaw would fall right off my face onto the floor and roll out into Walter's disco-themed lobby.

It was exactly the feeling you have when you almost drop your purse down a manhole in the city but instead you catch it just in the nick of time. My lower face muscles were like slippery, overcooked noodles.

"Holy cats, I'm a slack-jawed yokel!" I said, except it actually came out as: "Hory cas! I'n uh sack jawd yoko!"

"You're Yoko?" Walter eyed his nurse for an alternate translation. "Yoko Ono?" he guessed.

"It-gun-fa-off!" I insisted, cradling my chin in my hands. It felt as if it was hanging by mere threads connected to a space just above my ears. This couldn't be right, I thought. And if it was, it was *terrible*. It was so unnerving and I sounded like I'd had ten martinis. My whole face was a broken marionette.

"Your jaw? No, no! It's not going to fall off, you ridiculous girl."

"Ich ithh!" I said, panicked.

"It won't. Take your hands away and just try to open and close slowly."

I lowered my palms an inch away, still scared and not trusting. I let my mouth fall open slightly and then tried to bring my up teeth again. It was like doing a very slow pull up—only with my mouth. I felt my back teeth touch lightly and then slip slightly to the left. I still couldn't get my lips to meet and fully close.

"Try again," he said calmly.

Still holding my hands like a girl taking communion in church, I let my mouth fall open again, chin dropping, and Walter whipped out his tape measure to check the distance between my teeth. I could open about a half inch, but it felt like the Grand Canyon to me. I strained to do another chin-up. I could feel tears welling up. My lower jaw was shaking. As my back teeth came together, my upper and lower jawbones still felt like a pair of broken scissors with the blades misaligned and slipping crookedly past each other.

"I'm telling you, it's *not* going to fall off," Walter assured me.

"I owe . . . isss juss weir . . ." Translation: "I know, it's just weird."

This was so different from the aphasia I'd had with all my other seizures. I'd had my inner monologue back for months now. There was no straining of my brain scrambling and searching for the right words or trying to figure out how to sequence them. I had that down. It was the physical *mechanics* of speech and my mouth as an apparatus for communicating that I no longer had full command of.

At first, every word I tried to speak came out like water, a formless puddle of loose, risky vowels. *R* was probably the easiest noise to make before vowels. "Hello" came out *heyrro*. See you later became *Shee ew rater*. My tongue wasn't used to all the cavernous space it suddenly had to roam. Every thing tumbled out in overly rounded consonants and vowels. When frustrated, my words came out like scalpels with hard consonants erupting in singular, slicing cuts. I was a girl with Tourette's and a slightly inebriated slur. The most difficult sounds were any words with *B, F, V, P,* and *S. M*s were tough too. I got a referral for speech therapy.

Aᶠᵗᵉʳ ᵐᵒⁿᵗʰˢ ᵒᶠ ʳᵉᵖᵉᵃᵗᶦⁿᵍ "Bjorn Borg brings bravado to Bavaria with Bjork . . ." and "Sally sells seashells . . ." I was advised to try singing. I'd been in choir in high school and college—although I was never very good. I could carry a tune as a soprano, but I lacked power. The thing is I've always wanted to be a torch singer with a powerful, soulful Patti LuPone–style lounge act.

Because I'd also had considerable trouble with *m* sounds, I'd been doing this absurd monster song from *The Muppet Show*, the whole of which involved repeating "Manumanuh" to this chipper tune about a hundred times. I also practiced my super-villain laugh: "Mwah-hahahahahah." The most important thing seemed to be to keep the set list ever evolving. I'd been doing exaggerated renditions of Tom Jones's "What's New Pussy-cat" around the house because it requires so many facial muscles and types of sounds from hard to soft. But I knew I needed to mix things up to keep the neighbors from going bonkers.

There were multiple times, though, after being unwired by Walter, where my mouth and jaw would stop working alto-gether. Just like that, with very little warning, the muscles would abruptly freeze up and clamp shut. When this would happen I couldn't even speak in Hepburnese! What's it like to be mute in Manhattan—the city that never sleeps, the city that never stops talking, the city that's always irate? No one knows how to process you. They're expecting you to match and reciprocate their level of angst, and when you can't, things get ridiculous fast.

It happened without warning, on the subway. I was standing there holding my little square-inch section of the pole, trying not to be an inconsiderate manspreader. The train was already packed body-to-body by Forty-Second Street. Sandwiched between a Melania Trump drag queen and a nun, I was getting close to my stop when this very zaftig blind woman steps onto the train. She held her cane close to her person as her male companion stepped on beside her. They both lingered in the doorway—the only open space left in the packed car.

My station was coming up and so I was trying to subtly make a move toward the door to indicate that I was getting off. I nudge and nudge and lower my head to push forward, but no one seems to get it. I try to speak in the blind woman's general direction, "Ggghuu . . ." but my mouth won't comply. It simply won't make the words "Getting off" or "Excuse me." The hard *G* is a great, mostly closed-teeth sound, by the way.

"What's happenin'?" The blind woman whispered up over shoulder to her friend, clearly sensing my agitation. "Is somebody tryin' to saying somethin'?"

As I wiggled and wiggled toward the now-open but still mostly blocked doors, her friend whispered "Not sure," zeroing in on me with a furrowed brow like I was a girl off her meds. Behind him, an ominous sign instructed New Yorkers sternly, "See Something. Say Something."

Inside my head, the polite but still pushy-jerky girl was pleading now: Getting off! Excuse me! Pardon me? Hello???

How can you *not* understand me? But my mouth was still not cooperating, so it was just saying, "Ecusss . . ."

With the subway doors open, a few skinny bodies twisted and turned past the blind lady and her friend to make their escape. I made my own futile efforts but was still pressed up against Melania and couldn't move my arms. "Looks like she's trying to say something," the friend added.

And I realized what they were expecting from me was a truly irritated, "Get the fuck out of the way, so people can get off!" But I could no longer do that sort of thing. I just didn't have it in me that day or most days.

The doors closed. The train departed my stop. I resolved to get off next at Ninety-Sixth Street and walk back down, but I couldn't help but laugh at the situation. Here are two women, a blind one and a mute one, just trying to manage a single public interaction. Two people who needed to communicate in a clear and immediate way but couldn't: the blind woman and her friend were trying to translate my angst, meanwhile strangers were chuckling to themselves at the three of us—trying to give our misunderstanding some privacy. And I think now about how much the world needs to adapt for this. How we need to become translators for a broadening spectrum of difference and disability. The new motto needs to be, See something. Say something. But if you can't, subway charades are a perfectly acceptable way to bridge communication.

A S PART OF LEARNING how to smile again, there was a time where I would spend long stretches holding a pencil level between my teeth while doing everyday tasks like the dishes or vacuuming. I also had to say the word *pink* a hundred or so times a day. It uses all the smile muscles. My hope was that in six months' time, I might look less like Johnny Depp always sneering. Without language, I was paying attention to the world in a new way. They say 70 percent of overall communication is nonverbal and dependent on facial gestures, but I still didn't even have those back yet. To be able to smile, even a little and more evenly across both sides of my face, would be a huge step.

I also had to spend a fair amount of time each day pretending I was talking to a dog: "Who's a good boy? Who's a good boy?" I sounded so insanely exaggerated that even Marilyn asked if we'd gotten a new dog. It was ridiculous, but I needed that level of emotion and excitement to try to drive feeling back into my lips. I was missing being able to feel a kiss.

During the time when I was mostly mute, wouldn't you know it, *everyone* would talk to me. I remember, I was trudging up Madison Avenue to the dentist in the freezing rain for what must have been my nine millionth root canal (that I still cannot afford) when a man came right up to me and said, "Can I just tell you, I *really* like your boots!"

The snarky jerk in my head replied, "Well then, I *clearly* need to do some shopping because these boots are from Costco, mister. That's right, the brand is 'waterproof.'" But instead out loud all I said was, "Thank you," which actually came out as, "Hank hue."

Then he launched into his pitch. He and his wife were living in a homeless shelter with a newborn baby. In my desire to be empathetic, I totally forgot that I still couldn't make the right faces. I could *only* look either terrified or very cynical. I must have looked really scared because a cabbie stopped traffic on Madison and called out to me, "Hey, are you okay?! Is he bothering you?"

And lo, in a voice that came out in my first fully formed intelligible words in months, I called back, "No, he just likes my footwear!"

Holy fuck! I sounded mostly like me for the first time since "the big one"! A total stranger's pretext of liking my mediocre boots had just given me back my words. I gave him my only dollar left in nickels—the housing situation in the city is really the worst—but it made me think more than ever about how we need to proceed thoughtfully, with compassion for those who are wired differently from how we are. You just never know who might turn out to be a pal.

As I stood there in the doorway now with Marilyn and Biscuit, I heard myself and she was right. My speech was better. Then, she leaned forward and said, "You know, if you just put your top teeth on top of your bottom lip like you're a simpleton with buck teeth you will *totally* nail the 'Fuck off.'"

14

Get Your Freak On

TELLING THE PERSON you like or even love that you have epilepsy is hard, or at least it was for me. I could hear Loïc saying it now, in his very serious, very incredulous Frenchy voice: "Oh, but *mon amour*! You are a genetic *cauchemare*!" (French for nightmare.)

I knew I wasn't the girl for Loïc. Unless a doctor also surgically removed my conscience, it would be a mistake to get any more attached and not tell him. I'd gotten very good at hiding my epilepsy for a while. I hid both my pills and my auras. I swore everyone in life to secrecy, but I'd known it was only a matter of time before he either found out or I 'fessed up. We had met the year before, in 2014. He had never been married and still wanted kids. I already had two that I wasn't taking enough care of these days. I had to admit it: I *was* a genetic nightmare. To be an already childish grown-up with epilepsy, possibly parenting a new child who might be predisposed to epilepsy, depression, and anxiety seemed unimaginably hard and unfair to both him and any subsequent people we might make. It was over.

Even before seizures and epilepsy, dating had been hard enough. For one, I had never been good at reading social cues. I am a nerd, and if I had been born a boy, I would have probably fallen in with the *Dungeons and Dragons* computer kids and been constantly bullied by the big, scary jocks. And even when I did manage to grow out of my awkward *Edward Scissorhands* teen years and into my cuter, more grown-up face and self, I still had terrible luck dating.

Prime example: back in my midtwenties, I once went out on a blind date with an older guy who took me to see *Schindler's List*. I was just trying to say goodnight and totally ugly-crying in the doorway of my little West Village studio and telling him that I was too sad to ever see him again. Thank you for the sushi. Goodnight . . . sob, sob, sob. No, you can't come in. Besides, I'm not into the midlife crisis set.

With marriage, I had never known such relief. Finally, no more telling your story to new people—you had your person, your favorite entertainment in all the world, you didn't even need to go anywhere or have any money. You could just stay home all day and have sex and play house. I would have lived in a tent with my first husband. Forget sushi. Forget *Schindler's List*. I had finally found a degree of nerd who complemented my exact degree of nerd. What's more . . . I believed in him, in his novel, his writing, and his brain to the nth degree. I believed in all his dreams. He just didn't believe in mine and that's not his fault at all. I think I would have divorced me too. I was a jerk. I'd been so frantic to save both girls from having anything but a normal, perfect life. During that time, my remodeling and redecorating took on a decidedly aggressive tone. I don't know how anyone put up with me. I scraped so much wallpaper and flipped so many houses, I am probably responsible for the US housing crash.

But dating as a single mother is even worse than dating as a never-married woman. Yes, you know a little more about the deal breakers, the things you can live with, things you absolutely cannot abide. But when you have children, you have so much at stake, so much to protect. You don't want to harm a single hair on their little emotional heads. You've already done that to a certain extent if you've split up and had to move and change schools. It's a lot for tiny, delicate hearts to process. I didn't want to inflict any more damage than had already been done.

I decided to keep things "church and state" when it came to dating and the kids. My heart was broken. I couldn't conceive of life without my ex-husband. Maybe he was my life's big love and that was it. In my mind, we had been through too much together to throw it all away. Still, I knew I needed to heal and figure how we were going to be a *Gilmore Girls*–style household, so the most important thing was to have rules. Here's what I came up with:

No introductions. I was not introducing them to anyone unless I absolutely knew he was a person who could go the distance. This would not be a Disney movie where the kids would be peeking out the upstairs window as Mom's new friend arrived to pick her up for a date. If I were going to be dating anyone ever again there would have to be a lot of vetting off-site. Background checks, references, lab work, and so on. I would meet the person at the restaurant in my own car. There would be no nightcaps. I didn't want my kids getting attached to anyone who wasn't anything but a friend. I didn't want there to be any male "friends" hanging around. It just seemed wrong. Plus, I know my children and they're rascals. I didn't want them scaring off any truly worthy candidates. That was my department. They still managed to one-up me on this front one time. I was on a date and they locked the nanny out of the house with her phone and told her she couldn't come back inside unless she called me and said to come home right that instant. Needless to say, I made my excuses and cut the dinner short.

No overnight guests. I'd decided on no grown-up sleepovers unless I ever met someone and things got super serious. If there were going to be trysts en route to getting shack-up-together serious, they would have to be at the prospective person's house and not at my house when my kids were around. It would be too nerve racking and confusing—at least until everyone was much older. Myself included. This sort of worked for a while. Then, it didn't—but that can come in another book.

So, dating was already complicated enough without factoring in a chronic condition, especially when the SMMMs (smug, mean, married moms) already thought you wanted to bed their doughy, boring husbands. Trust me, we don't. I don't. So that was another rule. Only date the fully divorced, knowing that their standard line is, "She was crazy. I just couldn't take it anymore and I'm so lonely." No, no, no. This was already a bad narrative that rarely ended well for the woman.

With the diagnosis and subsequent seizures, dating changed yet again. All the forums and articles I'd read about dating with a chronic condition said to wait to tell the person when there's a foundation established. The problem is that I am a *terrible* liar. My face (at least before I broke it) showed every fib, every fab (this is a really *big* lie), every half truth, every whole truth, and every well-intentioned white lie. Before epilepsy I would have made the worst spy. Every emotion just showed up, plain as day. But when it comes to dating with epilepsy, suddenly you feel like every potential relationship is beginning with a lie, like you're carrying around this deep, dark secret. You have this big, scary vulnerability that is your ultimate kryptonite. If you are a really crappy liar as I am and you happen to think you might really like the person, you just want to take your glasses off like Clark Kent longs to do with Lois Lane and confess right then that really you're a spaz. Hiding such a big thing can feel like such a massive omission on your transcript.

So, do you confess? Do you just come right out and spill the brain beans? What hints can you drop along the way that might lessen the impact, the crushing blow of the news? Maybe they could already tell? You don't have to necessarily adopt the persona of "Angry Ep Truther," even if you are a little that way. If you wait until you've established a baseline of mutual trust, where he (or she) has shared some information about himself of equal proportion, it doesn't have to be so bad—even if you are a genetic *cauchemare*.

My diagnosis brought with it a sustained fatalism—the knowledge that I might not wake up if the next time I seized had an odd effect. I no longer clung to life as I used to, which was kind of a huge game changer for a chronic worrier. I reasoned that if I wasn't going to wake up, I might as well go out satisfied. I was a horny motherfucker with the impulse control of a toddler. Oh, the promiscuities!

My forties should have been about fighting off decay and the slow, sordid demise of my fuckability, but I think less about this now. The whole face rebuilding, learning to speak again, and getting seizure-free has distracted me. Epilepsy had me so scared that I would never find love again, at least not on any consistent basis with a single person I could stand. I suppose I could grandly pronounce, "Behold me in all my glory as an old, whitey spinster!" but the thing of it is, all of it has added up to be the best douchebag detector ever: my epilepsy, my slightly shifted face. I've also come to a time of life where getting your "freak" on starts taking on a whole new meaning, in that it's about finding the equal freak to your freak, the person who refuses to behave in the same way you refuse to behave. It's more a partners in crime slow burn than any rush of infatuation.

Telling someone you have something chronic like epilepsy, someone you think you might love and who might love you, can feel like pulling off Grandma's nightcap and revealing that you're the wolf. The person might scream, and you very well might howl, revealing a perfectly crooked grin, whereupon the person might kiss you. Or flee. It happens. We are, after all, not our mates.

It's tricky because in revealing yourself so personally on such a fundamental, molecular level, you immediately shove the person right into a very gray area, one that generally shuts most guys up. Yes, you've gone on several dates and maybe even accepted a gift, you've made out with the person, felt around each other's curves and contours. There's no way after you tell him (or her) you're a spaz (or fill in your blank) that his next move won't be personal. It definitely will be—because you took a risk and revealed your biggest vulnerability. If his next decision doesn't become specifically about you and wanting to understand more of what epilepsy means, he winds up looking like a super-shallow jerk. It's hard and awkward, because you just hope the person will be better than they sometimes are. Any relationship worth being in usually comes with some complexity and angst. Everyone has something they're grappling with even if it's not readily apparent. You may not have epilepsy, but you've got a racist granny or a jailbird brother-in-law. Don't be fooled. No one is not dealing with something at some point. And if the person does react negatively at first or feel betrayed, it's not to say they'll stay that way. People need to be taught how to see us, how to respond and live with us.

The person may have noticed from your house that you have something medical going on, some more complex backstory than you've let on. I once had a boyfriend who mistook me for poor because my bed was on the floor. It had nothing to do with solvency at the time and everything to do with worrying about falling out of bed midseizure/midsex. I slept on a frameless mattress and had only rounded, padded corners throughout my house.

There is a deep, intransient weirdness of simply being a woman with epilepsy, a person who is electric. Now there is always a third person in the room, in the bed, and at the table. Seizures, as with most things chronic, tend to bring on some degree of sexual chaos. You need to be willing to embrace total abjection—neither subject nor object—because you, the spaz, are something in the middle. It may turn you into the butt of someone's joke, but perhaps your true kink lies in tricking yourself into being vulnerable and open enough to the threesome that is you, your partner, and epilepsy. Then, suddenly, there you are, looking like you've been struck by lightning and are dying over your white wine spritzer. Everything can feel very high stakes. "What if you seize while we're in the middle of things? What do I do?" he might venture. "Does ardent lovemaking bring on this sort of thing?" he asks timidly. "What if I accidentally kill you?"

"You won't. And if you did, *I* certainly won't have any idea about it. I'll be dead. If epilepsy kills me, it's on science to figure out. For my part, given how gorgeous my seizures can be, it might not be the worst way to go." Not everyone is up for an answer like that and so you end up having to get over a lot of relationships that never were, relationships you imagined going somewhere, because people are simply scared and seizures break all social contracts. But again, it's a great douchebag detector.

Then there's the friend zone: we're so filled with longing as human beings. You just want to lie in the bed with someone, to feel close in a way you haven't in ages. Boys *always* employ this line, so it's even more suspicious when it comes out of a girl's mouth. It is the line of every nice guy negotiating to spend the night, and then you find yourself making up excuses and half-seriously speaking in the patois of consent by referencing the respecting of boundaries and keeping your clothes on.

While I haven't had a tonic-clonic seizure in eighteen months, my brain will never be "normal." It will always control my life in ways other people can't even imagine. Anxiety in grocery stores and Martinson coffee is still a factor, but it doesn't define me as much anymore. It's no longer the first thing I tell workout buddies; friends can be around me for months before they notice or ask about my strange sleeping habits. I have made a religion of bedtime. It's simply the same rites with the same pills at the same time. Lack of sleep is probably my biggest seizure trigger. I still sleep more than anyone I know. It makes me boring, all these naps, but I no longer care what people think, so much.

My condition and my meds are slowly becoming something people gradually realize about me rather than something I stress about them needing to know right at the get-go. I school them gently in a do–re–mi of to-dos should I ever have a seizure in their company. I tell them how my mind begins to float and swarm, like fireflies in a jar. It's a "shit's going to go down" panic that tells me to get to a safe place. A soft place. There's the shimmer and I'll feel like a current is rising up and passing through the top of my head, glowing, and flying out my eyes while I lie on the bed or the ground. "I'm buzzing," I'll say and then of course I'll be unsure how to follow up the phrase. What can I say to help the person understand? A shallow exhale of anxiety is what you have come to anticipate and expect. Sometimes I'm convinced that no other person will ever know my electric brain the way I do and that I'll always be on my own because of it.

But unless it's the right freak for my freakish self, maybe it's not so bad. In this way, love becomes terribly self-selecting. Those too afraid take themselves out of the equation. Those curious enough tend to stay.

15

I Feel Bad About My Face

"OKAY, MS. JONES, now if you could just try to look as deformed as possible . . ." the nurse coached me from behind the camera as I gawped. "Oh, that's perfect!" The camera shutter clicked.

"But . . . I didn't do anything!"

"Oh, oh! Do that again!" More fervent shutter clicking.

This was the most surreal photo shoot I'd ever been witness to. I attempted a full-scale Quasimodo expression by smiling with the part of my face that remained working—the area around the left corner of my lip and eye. Still, it was necessary if the insurance was going to cover the reconstructive procedures to retrofit the pieces of my face back together on a finer level and restore feeling. I'd been into the office for several meetings. My new boss in New York had recently all but told me that since the accident I was too ugly to come to client meetings. "They won't be comfortable doing business with you across the table" was, I believe, how he put it.

"I'm pretty sure you can't say that." I told him, in my best Waspy-Connecticut accent.

"You're a contractor. I can say whatever I want," he shot back.

And he was right. As a contract creative director, he could cancel my gig at any time for any reason he deemed appropriate. I had to get back to feeling and looking like the person whom people (even the jerks) recognized and knew. Still, I was so crazily down about the comment, I'd started half-jokingly referring to myself as a deformed girl in private. Ed had grown so irritated with me, he threatened to make a swear jar for my face. The rule was every time I mentioned how freakish, deformed, and/or asymmetrical I looked, I'd have to put a dollar in the jar—except by then I was almost totally out of money, so technically I would end up owing the jar, which we decided would make me even sadder.

I really needed to return to work full time. More importantly, I needed to *feel* like myself again. I still only had sensation from the very top of my cheeks up to my hairline.

The first weeks home from the hospital had not gone quite as I'd anticipated. For starters, I was really weak. Like seriously, old-cat-lady-with-a-walker weak. I shuffled around the apartment sucking down smoothies and finely pureed soups through a straw. I never seemed to be able to get enough calories into my person for everyday life, so I still slept fifteen hours daily. I think in my damaged aftermath I expected everything to go much faster and align with the pace of the city, especially now that I was back in my own bed. With the girls both away at school and at their dad's, the joint would be quiet and I would bounce back from this little crisis, I kept telling myself.

Yes, I loved my little hovel of an apartment right next to the park with its overly large refrigerator, its floor-to-ceiling bookcases, and windows that opened out onto an overflowing jungle of a back garden. There was a green velvet chesterfield sofa that my friend Li helped me pick out, my striped overstuffed reading chair where I could lounge for hours, both legs hung over the arm. There were big chalkboards on the walls of the tiny kitchen for random ideas whenever they sprang up. Right in the heart of the 'hood, this apartment was ever so bright and calm in the back rooms. And there were so many birds. A symphony of finches and whippoorwills. Still, I nearly killed myself with a first post-op sneeze at home alone. The dust in the place was like a thick coat of frosting on Sophie's old turntable and all the surfaces, but I took comfort in the sameness of things, the small things that had *not* changed. I'd been told the healing would be neither progressive nor linear. It would be an awkward slog of crawling an inch forward one day only to slip back five the next. One day my chin might feel like it was being stabbed with a dozen knives; the next day I might lose all sensation and be drooling like a Labrador. I just hadn't imagined it would be more than a few weeks, or as carnivalesque as it was turning out to be.

Initially, there was the "fate" phase of healing: the unavoidable, predestined, and decidedly monstrous facial swelling the doctors had warned me about. It happens in the wake of this type of surgery, where you first look like a helium-inflated cartoon of yourself. This set in for me just before I came home from the hospital, but it's one of those things where you tend to look like someone has taken your face off its scaffolding, rolled it out like a piecrust, reattached it at your hairline, and then blown it up like the Stay Puft Marshmallow Man. I studied myself constantly during those first days, keeping watch for any infinitesimal sign of improvement. Overall, my mug was vaguely triangle shaped. Between the cranial stiches, cuts, and bruises, I was full of random holes and irregular patterns.

Then, as if by slow magic, my face started to shift like a Scooby-Doo villain mask deflating. It's the kind of thing where you just don't believe your body can actually make those kinds of wild, implausible Picasso-esque shapes. Originally, I had only thought that a mother's baby belly could grow to such a size. My mug was literally the elephant in the room. I felt so strikingly at odds with nature and so in contradiction with the rest of my skinny wimp of a frame. Yet somehow, my face, in growing against itself in order to heal, still managed to come up with all kinds of wacky geometry that was, in essence, *more me* than me at the time. And so, as with birth, you just hope you have the requisite amount of chemicals, muscle memory, collagen and whatever-else hormones are needed to make everything you are seeing (and feeling) go back to the way it was before. (Please face, please?)

You might think the worst part of breaking your face is the surrealist swelling or the grotesquerie of stink that comes from not being able to brush the *insides* of your teeth and tongue for a whole straight week at a time, or the fact that after a steady, monthlong diet of too-sweet smoothies and Jell-O cups, you hunger like a dying vampire for the taste, the texture, of salty medium-rare meat. I got so desperate one night, I thought, "Bitches gotta eat," so I ordered a bacon double cheeseburger from Jackson Hole on the Upper West Side, ground it to bits with a hand blender, and tried to suck it through a straw like some kind of mad beast with no real mouth to speak of. It was food torture porn of the worst kind.

No, the worst, pettiest, most annoying bit was when the pressure bandages came off. It wasn't just that I was totally beaten up and still bearing stitches and cranial staples; it was that I had actually developed a massive zit underneath the bandages. And I hadn't even felt it coming. Without being able to feel my chin, I had no more *zitvoyance*. This had previously been one of my special powers: the uncanny clairvoyant ability to anticipate and fend off bouts of adult acne. Talk about adding insult to injury. *Not* cool, body. I mean, I was already pretty torn up as it was. Give a girl a break, why don't you? Anyway, I immediately attacked that sucker with Neosporin cream; this is my only middle-aged acne wisdom that I bequeath to you all and I'm sure it's been proffered elsewhere on the Internet. (1) Don't ever break the skin. Don't squeeze things as, (a) that's gross, and (b) it just introduces infection. (2) Slather that cystic-zit-nightmare-about-to-happen in Neo cream—not the greasy clear stuff, the white cream. The next day, I usually find things have improved or gone away altogether.

Next came the "fury" phase of healing where you look like a longshoreman who has come home from a drunken pub brawl. The deep swirling bruises on my face and neck were like a lava lamp with an ever-shifting liquid interior that ranged from licorice black to angry purple, to a slow fade to sickly puce. Now matter how much I tried to smile or look neutrally indifferent, I still looked wild, sneering, and childishly sinister—like something only Maurice Sendak could dream up. I had resting beast face. My jaw and one tooth still jutted out to the left. The bones in my head and face still felt cracked in pieces, like a broken terra-cotta vase that had been gingerly Scotch-taped back together—with pins and plates. I worried things would all fall apart, so I wore this tight, little gray stocking cap because it felt comforting—as though it would hold all the still-loose bones in place until they grew back together.

After this came the "phantom" phase, where you are just haunted with pain and odd facial sensations for what seems like an eternity, a glacial age. The doctors had said neuropathy or nerve damage might be a factor in my recovery. Think numbness, constant tingling, stabbing sensations, tightness, muscle weakness, and a lack of movement. That said, this was more than anyone bargains for as, one by one, your tiny electric nerves literally *do* light up and start working again in the most unexpected ways. It's just the body healing, growing against itself, and the inflammation that happens in the wake of trauma, surgery, and regeneration. Still, it was like having a poltergeist living just under the surface of my skin, zipping around, making mischief, and occasionally wreaking havoc only to go all quiet. One day might find me waking to searing heat throughout my cheeks; another day my lips would be ice cold. Still, others might have me feeling like someone was actively stabbing knives into my whole face. My talking was still limited to a few hours, but if I overdid things, my face, jaw, and mouth would suddenly go on strike and clamp shut altogether, even after all the wires and bands came off.

Aside from the occasional conference call with work, not much got done. I ordered groceries online, communicated mostly on text and messenger with coworkers, and sent out the laundry. Friends brought things by and helped with errands, but I lived in a quiet mode I'd never really experienced before. It was a decidedly small and contained day-to-day existence.

Despite the neuropathy, the really bad, bad news that had been repeatedly explained to me in the hospital was that the nerves on the right side of my face, which fan out like daisy petals from the ear to the center of the face, had been very compromised and all but severed. This meant that everything from the middle of my forehead swooping past my cheekbones and on down to my chin was paralyzed with little to no sensation. This would most likely be permanent. On the plus side, I would have no wrinkles or frown lines resulting from normal facial muscle movement as I could neither frown nor smile. I had "perma-brood." My right eye drooped—similar to how a stroke patient's might. I was most sad about this because having no expression made me feel completely geriatric and as if no one would ever really understand me again. My face was so much a part of my emotional life and well-being. I could still blink—but only slowly and not very frequently. To save itself from self-ruin, my right eye would involuntarily rebel against properly looking straight ahead and roll back into my head. Admittedly, I looked a bit demonic when it would do that, but it was super quick. Like a demon flash! A shazam! of electricity zapped my eye over and over again. At one point, Walter took a picture to catch it and there was (briefly) a question of whether they would need to sew my lid shut to prevent permanent corneal damage. Walter would nag. Was I irrigating it enough? Was I wearing my pirate patch every night? The answer was an unqualified "yes." I had practically bedazzled my patch as I needed to be able to go back to work pronto.

That said, this time of "getting better" seemed to stretch out interminably like clouds on a windless day, imperceptibly creeping across the sky. It simply didn't occur to me that I wouldn't get better within a few weeks. I couldn't comprehend any other story than getting better. I had always bounced back from my previous seizures, and I was doing all the right things: loads of facial pushups where I'd work at actively raising the entire right side of my face in total hyperbolic alarm over and over again, including my dead eyebrow up toward my right ear and forehead. I practiced making fish-kiss faces and whistling constantly. To get feeling back in my lips, I would walk around the apartment making farty noises with my lips like French men do when they're making excuses for not doing things like the dishes or taking out the garbage. I was also blowing big raspberries in every direction.

In this way, I found that when something like this happens, you start to want to become the monster you resemble. And why shouldn't I? Maybe it's that ferocity that would help me lick this. I was gross, but I just needed to go with it. I would roar around the living room against my jaw wiring and, well, I liked it. "Let the wild rumpus start!" I would tell myself. This is how I would get better.

Though I was cognitively fine to return to writing pithy doo-dads and dealing with media partnerships, apparently I was still too horrific to be seen by our clients. After a few weeks I didn't have a black eye or bruising anymore. However, I did still have a pretty Jay Leno-esque chin—which looks fine on Jay Leno but was not so much what people were used to on me. I also didn't feel right. It was as though I was still trapped under the ice and muzzled with a kind of invisible duct tape.

I was not entirely "out" to Jeremy, my boss in New York. Things were still too new and I worried he would feel betrayed by having hired an epileptic. It was an all-male, conservative crew. A squad of Don Drapers and I was Peggy—at least before this particular seizure I was. But now, I really *did* scare the poor grocery delivery guy judging by the terrified look on his face. And it's true, my neighbor Pablo did *not* recognize me in the hallway and asked me if I was new to the building, but I needed to work, to feel like some normalcy was still possible.

By the time I did go back, I still had the phantom chin. It felt enormous, as if I'd been shot full of Novocain, and I still had these razor-sharp rubber bands holding my upper and lower teeth together, so I kept the chitchat to a minimum.

My boss wasn't having it. I was told I should consider disability, but the thing is, I didn't *feel* disabled. Everything worked in my head. In fact, on this new epilepsy drug that Delia had prescribed, which I still can't pronounce at all, I felt better than ever. I wasn't having auras. There was no "seizury" tinge to my days, no vertigo. The floor no longer throbbed like an immense alien heart. Gone was the supercharged electric buzzing in my brain. Best of all, I felt *awake*. There was no gauzy-gray veil to life these days. The cracks in the sidewalks and the wrinkles on people's faces were crisper than ever. *I* was crisp and clear. Indeed I felt crisp on *the inside*. On the outside, however, I made people uneasy with my bionic face still swollen and full of titanium. But to lose my job finally was rough. They called me at home to cancel my contract. Budget cuts was the official reason, but I knew. I was so angry I could spit—except I couldn't. Crying just made my whole face ache even more. Dumb mucous membranes. How was I going to do this? It would be another year before many of the pins and plates could be removed, but it was clear that if I was going to be allowed back into the work world, I would need to create the illusion of greater symmetry and work like freaking Eliza Doolittle on my diction—STAT as the surgeons say.

S O, THERE I WAS NOW with the plastic surgeon's nurse taking pictures, awkwardly exaggerating my deformed self—so that I might qualify for a procedure that would move me an inch back over the line of social and corporate acceptability. To do this, I needed the right side of my face to behave a little more like the left side. Both sides needed to droop in unison. If I couldn't smile symmetrically and evenly with my current muscles and nerve endings being in disarray, I could still look mildly bored and disgusted in order to fit back in with every other bored and disgusted colleague I might work with. I'd reasoned that would pass in New York City. I thought perhaps if I went from a resting freak face to resting bitch face, humanity might have me back.

At the same time, my jaw needed to relax to the right just a millimeter to keep from looking misaligned and shifty. There was nothing they could do about the swelling. My Jay Leno look would just take time to die down. In the meantime, I could hide it (partially) with the right haircut, tapered just enough to soften the jawline. Lastly, my eyes needed to appear mostly the same size and work in parallel with each other instead of the right one drifting up and looking dead. I would take a break from contacts and only wear my dark-frame nerd glasses from decades earlier. The glasses would distract. The rest would have to be improvised with Botox and fillers.

Now, you judge a plastic surgeon's office *not* by the binder of "before and after" photos but by their staff. Does the receptionist look a bit too surprised to see you? Does the treatment coordinator appear a little too tightly pulled and windblown from her last complimentary tuck? How are the necks? And what of the other supplicants in the waiting room? Were they just there for injectables? Did any of them have any serious structural and symmetry issues akin to yours? Were there any drooping eyes? Was there a jaw out of whack anywhere? I tried to peek at the other patients behind their magazines. Most of the women and one man seemed to be there for cosmetic maintenance. The smartness of their dress made me think they were probably a little fussier about everything than I was. Oh, how I missed the luxury of being fussy about little things. I would have given anything right about then for a simple marionette line (the parentheses-style wrinkles around your mouth) that could be quickly and easily filled with some Juvéderm. To even be able to both feel and wrinkle my forehead would be like savoring a big piece of cake with the best frosting ever.

Coco Chanel once said, "Nature gives you the face you have at twenty. Life shapes the face you have at thirty. But at fifty, you get the face you deserve."

Really Coco? I still have a few more years before I'm fifty, but did I *really* deserve this? Yes, I was wearing my spazzy electric brain plainly on the outside now, right on my face. That much was clear, but did I really deserve this was the wrong question to ask, I know. The greater question was what was I going to do with this face now?

Your face becomes an emotional map of your life. There is a wrinkle of regret, a side eye scowl of knowing a lie when you hear one, and the vertical lines above your lip from all those cigarettes you smoked with the other mothers on your mums' nights out. The smile lines from your marriage and what you believed was going to be a thoughtful, quirky life, well lived together. What happens when the map is almost entirely erased? Tabula rasa. Do you try to reconstruct the map as you and others remember it? Or do you draw new lines altogether? For my part, I just needed anything that looked like a map. That was my starting point: a basic human map with discernable human features, and then I figured nature could draw what it willed.

The Park Avenue plastic surgeon strode into the exam room with my chart. Dr. Henry was a bespectacled man in his early forties. Groomed within a molecule of his life, he had not a wrinkle in sight and yet he still looked human. In other words, he was not *too* unrealistically good looking. This was important to me because I didn't need to look perfect. I just needed to *pass* as unbroken enough for work, for my kids, for any sort of ordinary future. On the wall behind him, multiple Ivy League diplomas silently oozed credibility. He surveyed the chaotic landscape of my mug and then contemplated the X-rays, noting the amount of metal still lodged in my head. Of the paralysis on the right side of my face, the best they could do was to try to balance things out by paralyzing portions of the left side with Botox. This would also help my eyes to appear more symmetrical. They couldn't do anything about the fleeting moments when my eyeball rotated up into my head—that would just take time—but they could even out the droop across both eyes. They would need to do a number of strategic injections in my upper jaw, face and scalp. *No problemo*, I thought. I wasn't afraid of shots after everything I'd just been through. I'd had my whole face taken off and put back on. Shots were easy. What I was most afraid of was pity, of not being able to support my family, of being a lost cause and being entirely unlovable in any shape or form for the rest of my days. I was more afraid of that than the seizures themselves.

To get the insurance to cover the symmetry fixes he was recommending, Dr. Henry reiterated that they would need to submit the photos we were taking today to prove the deformity was significant enough to warrant the procedures. Then, he paused a moment to counsel me that I was getting older and presumably wiser now. Given what had happened to me, I should consider myself lucky to be alive. I could have broken my neck or been paralyzed. Shouldn't I consider myself above and beyond such trivialities as symmetry? He told me I needed to get comfortable with the idea of inner beauty.

I would have gasped if I'd been able. What the hell was happening here? The guy whose very industry had trained the world to value symmetry and classic external beauty norms was selling *me* on inner beauty? Was this all some sort of sadistic prank? What was most annoying was I couldn't even raise my eyebrows in shock at his patronizing tone. I indulged in an invisible eye roll. In a world where one's face, beauty, and even identity are governed by laws that embrace order, pattern, symmetry, and simplicity, I still felt like utter chaos. I was a creature from *Where the Wild Things Are*. Yes, the splotches of yellow and purple had faded, but I was still misshapen on the inside and out.

Add to that, New York is a city of reaction, a city of critics, columnists, and great pontificators. Everybody, down to the very last little old lady at your optometrist's office who tightens the screws on your glasses, has an opinion. They all have a clear and pronounced reaction to everything and anything. Everyone here reacts. The more they like something, the more irritated and loud they get about it. Everyone except me. I had nothing. I couldn't smile. I couldn't fully frown. I couldn't look angry. My teeth still didn't meet when I would bite down. My words were still limited to a few hours a day before all of my face muscles became tired and I started to sound like a lush. I had no expression, no symmetry, no proportion, and no sensation, which meant I could easily burn myself if I didn't touch-test all of my warm liquids and foods. I also could never tell if I had food all over my face. When I would hang out with Ed or Holly, I would jokingly smear things across my chin, then gesture to my whole visage and ask, "How am I doin'?" because it was the only way I knew how to manage the awkwardness of all of these little moments.

And while things shifted slightly every day, the overarching healing process had been *so* incremental in pace. I needed some agency in all this. *Not* to be lectured. Where I'd felt mostly beautiful before (both inside and out) now I felt like Kirk Douglas. My "resting freak face" resembled a stroked-out male movie star with a droopy eye and an overly pronounced jawline. Not that there's anything wrong with that—strokes happen to the best of us. I knew I needed to get stronger, but I was still your average vain forty-something-year-old lady who just wanted to worry about simple things like crow's feet and not having overly surprised eyebrows. I admit it. I like shallow. Shallow is fine. Shallow doesn't require me to become a better person. Still, I felt like a living, breathing, Botox-nuclear accident. Now this good-looking doctor guy was lecturing me on inner beauty? (Cue unbridled shrieking.)

The nurse came back in with the camera and we shot more deformed pictures. Yes, I was older and wiser now—probably. Yes, I was lucky to be alive—probably. Yes, I was well versed in the idea of inner beauty and had tried to instill that concept in my daughters, but guess what? Our world isn't versed in it. Our world is judgmental and discriminatory and full of douchebags at work. I still needed to participate in the workplace as best as I could. But most of all, what my sage wisdom was telling me was that it was still *my* face. The one accessory I couldn't just take off. And I still cared about it and I wanted to feel better about it—even if it was a spazzed-out face. Plus, it's not up to Dr. Henry to school me on inner beauty. Because guess what? I was *already* pretty enough on the inside and *plenty* in love with myself, thank you very much.

"Okay, smile now!" said the nurse.

INDIGNITY ASIDE, I *did* worry about my face rigidity, that the muscle might seriously atrophy and somehow become gangrenous. I supposed I could handle a crooked spaz face, but not a zombified one. I kept up with the exercises and kept checking in with Walter, my original surgeon who was right in the neighborhood. Something *had* to work. Possibly brain-damaged by electricity and exhaustion, I could not make sense of *any* other kind of story than this. I could not make sense of not getting better—of being able to smile, feel a kiss, and chew my food without pain. If I couldn't totally fix me, that would be tough. I would have to adjust, but in the meantime, I could still teach/ show the people around me that I was *still me*—still alive in there, underneath all the invisible duct tape and misshapen titanium bits. I guess this is the part where I should also tell you that the dentist couldn't fix my broken teeth until my jaw was free of the bands and wiring. I had a ways to go before any of this could happen, and I might be a less chatty girl for the time being, but *I* was still there, I insisted. That was me on a good day.

On a bad day, a sidelong glance in the living room mirror would hollow out my chest with deep, muddy despair. I didn't want anyone to see what my overly electric brain had done to me or what heinous thing it had made me into. I felt such feral shame. On a bad day, the depression that set in after the job loss was such a brow-beating, fickle, vitriolic bitch. Imagine you have a very dramatic actress—like Glenn Close—playing a kind of emotional vampire on stage in your head. She waltzes onto the scene deftly manipulating, draining your every feeling, and then magnifying all your fears and anxieties without missing a beat. A bunny-boiling rage monster; that's what this depression was. My grand, grand mal seemed my life's defining failure. Sadness at this failure would well up in my gullet when I was alone, and nest there. It was a lump in my throat that I couldn't resolve or talk out. I had no words.

And it wasn't just that people I knew didn't recognize me. Often *I* didn't recognize me. Who was that melted, crooked-looking girl? And *what* happened to her teeth? Was she born that way? Or was it an accident? Must have been a doozy. The human brain has evolved into such an efficient storyteller. I could see strangers working out in seconds that something was wrong with me, but I didn't yet have the voice, the teeth, or the social cues to convince them otherwise. I withdrew to my head for a time. I stopped trying to explain. I retreated socially and professionally. I stopped trying to be back in the world, pretending that everything was fine.

Can you be homesick for your face? Can you be filled with so much longing for the self you used to be that you just don't want to "be" at all? Was this the same notion of loss of identity or loss of self that therapists always talked about? The kind endemic to chronic illness, where everything you know about yourself vanishes and so you have to build a new, different life with new rules and habits? I stopped going out so much. I haunted my apartment like a little ghost. Had so much of my identity really been bound up in my appearance as a woman? How much had been tied to my job? To motherhood? How much to my crazy family—who were all on the West Coast and dealing with their own dramas? How much in simply being able to speak clearly and be understood. Identity is a slippery notion at best even when you haven't had anything serious happen to you.

On a more practical level, in terms of working and making ends meet, would anyone new hire me now? All I wanted was to blend in and be "normal" by New York City standards, which you have to admit allows for a pretty broad spectrum of aesthetic and life choices. But there were days I felt I could never hide even in a city where I'd always felt relatively anonymous. Now perfect strangers would ask what was wrong with me. After responding a couple dozen times in my limited way, though, I realized that most people were not trying to make me feel bad. Usually, the opposite was true. Most people were just trying to connect and relate. A number responded with their own tales of how they had broken something or been in a car accident. There were also curious strangers who were just attempting to make sense of what was in front of them: a spaz, now both inside and out.

B UT THERE WAS WALTER once again poking me with small tines of a lobster fork. I had started to feel slightly more sensation in my cheeks on that week's visit.

"I miss lobster and beef . . . and pie," I told him, wistfully in my sloppy brogue. "When this is all over, I am going to eat a *whole* cow. Poor Bessie," I sighed.

But now, Walter was not laughing at me. He was alternating between poking me with the lobster fork and squinting at a single, ghostly X-ray. Then he said, "You realize, the break was right at the nerve, kiddo?"

He just looked at me, sorry. It was the same sorry, sad face of the EMT guy. Walter poked my lips again, and I wanted to tell him I *did* feel something, but I'd have been lying. He put his hand over my eyes, continuing to prod at different intervals and that's when I wondered pretty much out of nowhere, what if my last kiss was *really* my *last* kiss?

All these different things spun in my head. I'd imagined one day I'd look up, and blink, I'd be an old lady, but I hadn't imagined I would turn into a long-faced, lantern-jawed beast overnight. I avoided eye contact in public. I had to constantly remind myself to keep my lips together (which was still a challenge), so that I would not be perceived as a slacked-jawed, mouth-breathing idiot. Friends mostly treated me with white kid gloves—I could see they felt helpless to do anything. The best times though were when they would show up with something specific that would remind me of being me. To make speech therapy less tedious, my friend Billie got me a Shakespeare Insult Generator, which was a strange contraption of a book that provided hours of morally offensive phrasing that I could direct at my therapist. I could call her a loathsome-puke-stocking if I was in a particularly foul mood. Another friend donated some seriously amazing pro-bono dentistry and made me these insane margarita smoothies—with just a smidge of the good stuff on them.

I thought back to my last kiss with Loïc. In my imagination, I could still recall the nuances of it. There was nothing like a kiss. A kiss was better than the perfect warmth you felt at the first snow of the season, cool flakes falling soft on your cheeks, that I-cannot-get-you-close-enough feeling of yearning and satisfaction, of appetite and fulfillment, of holding someone's face in your hands. Taking in their magic as they take in yours. It was the wild rush of being consumed and consuming, of giving them the indescribable, extraordinary feeling of a deep, all-consuming kiss. I remembered my face in his hands. His in mine. The street corner in the East Village where we first kissed. *Never let that bit go*, I thought now in Walter's chair. That was my very unequivocal New York opinion, my manifesto for this lightning strike, this seizure. Keep your last kiss close and ever closer in case you don't get to feel it again.

Make certain your last kiss was your best kiss. Never take it for granted. Kiss your loved ones all the time. Before Loïc would leave the house in the mornings when we were still a *we*, I would kiss him like crazy—not just because I loved him or thought I loved him but because like any daffy Frenchman riding a bike in the city, he would wear one of those useless little Frenchy bike hats instead of a proper helmet. This made me crazy, and so I would say, "You realize you have a death wish?" and then force him to smooch and smooch and smooch until he would be legitimately late for work. But just in case he was hit by a bus and I never saw him again, I wanted him to feel totally, fully loved.

Walter uncovered my eyes now and told me plainly with nary a hint of drama that he needed to go back in again, rebreak my jaw, realign things, and address nerve issues. I wasn't healing right. But instead of peeling my face off my skull again, this time they would go in arthroscopically from the other side of my jaw, he told me, by my left ear. It wouldn't be nearly as bad as the first emergency surgery.

You may wonder why I wasn't completely devastated by this news, how it is I didn't start bawling right there in the chair in front of Walter and his nurse. My epilepsy had changed the way I went about things now. I think after six years of seizures you get used to everything being so unexpected and always being such an emergency that you relish any opportunity to plan anything. Last time had been a total life-and-death crisis—an oh-God-what-do-we-do-with-her? crisis. This time was like a massive do-over. Everybody in life wants a do-over—I certainly did. If Walter needed a do-over to get things right so I could feel again, I wasn't going to be sad about that. I was going to be hopeful.

Still, I groaned audibly as I considered going through it all once more: ugh, the gnawing morphine itch, the incalculable vulnerability of backless nighties. No matter how you tie them, they always fall open and show the part of your fanny you don't like most, which for me was all of it. The simple trick I learned from the nurses, because I am clueless when it comes to being sick or in the hospital, was to always ask for two gowns. The first one you put on so that it opens in the back like they ask, so that doctors can get all up in there if they need to. The second gown you put on backward over the first one and wear as a robe. How did I *not* know this?

Then, there was the prospect of being wired shut even longer. I *was* learning how to be a mute in the city and make it work. At least, I would be better prepared this time. I'd bring Bananagrams to play with Ed and the one cool nurse on the ward. There was always one. I'd sport better undies in the event of eligible doctors, maybe get a Brazilian wax that wasn't so spectacularly botched this time. I'd remember sour apple Jolly Ranchers and mints and sneak in better smoothies. Most of all, I would be ready.

To have my jaw broken again, however voluntary this time, seemed a cruel joke. I needed to stay funny right now because, oh boy, did I feel bad about my face.

HOME AGAIN AFTER AN eleven-hour surgery, I had been shuffling around my apartment having escapist real-estate fantasies and looking like a drunk lady, wearing a jockstrap on my chin. The procedure had been more of an ordeal than Walter had painted it. I'm not saying he was whitewashing it or anything. It's just that my face hadn't responded well to the retractors, which were the implements the surgeons used to open my mouth to get fully inside to realign my jaw. The swelling, after having stretched my face out so intensely, was unreal. (I have photos, but they're scary.)

Surgery felt like such violence. My whole body was exhausted from it. I was sleeping sixteen hours a day because it was the only time I didn't feel pain. That said, even if I was wired shut, unable to speak, and completely freakishly grotesque, I loved what my Percocet-addled brain was dreaming up: ideas about full-scale inner and outer makeovers—not just clothes, makeup, or hair—but an overall way of being.

The makeover is what the French philosophers called a "technology of the self"—a script or story through which we make sense of our identity. Maybe I needed a Frenchy makeover? I needed more joy to help break up this long slog of healing. Along with drinking Sancerre and cooking, I thought it might be wise to channel the French ladies. Their ideas on beauty might feel more authentic, more comfortable in one's skin, and less plastically pretty. I thought back to Jeanne Moreau in Luc Besson's film *La Femme Nikita* and the scene where Jeanne teaches a scrappy street junkie, played so beautifully (and subtly) by Anne Parillaud, how to be a woman. Maybe this was how I needed to reframe things?

Just what was their secret? French women seemed to do everything with an effortless *je ne sais whaaaaaa?* sort of way—whether it was dressing, dating, eating, or resisting brutal fascist dictators. How might I repurpose a few of their tactics to adapt to this new face of mine? I brainstormed in my little kitchen with my jaw-strap.

Flirt routinely as a matter of course. It's in every French woman's genetic makeup to flirt with anyone who shows up on her doorstep—*quel charme!* I do so love this expression. I'd guessed I might find such a tactic helpful when I felt misunderstood, was the recipient of disapproving glances, or possibly mistaken for being mentally ill or tipsy. To me, flirting was all in the eyes. If I couldn't smile with my mouth, maybe I could smile with my eyes? Or practice looking quizzical? I was getting better at blinking and directing my gaze with purpose.

Insist on highbrow core pieces. Given that I was now a spaz inside and out, I realized I needed to pay attention to all the key trappings of normalcy—including what I wore. It wasn't enough to zip out to the bodega in my torn-up jeans and old Jack Purcell's. While getting better, I couldn't risk having another seizure being mistaken for someone on drugs or mentally ill. I needed to lose the baubles and anything that might read as anything but what I was—a regular nerd-lady with a good eye for shoes and tailoring. French women have an innate gift for recognizing quality and buying things that last. Bye-bye fast fashion. Hello investment pieces that I would be happy to die in—or that would make anyone immediately intuit that I wasn't a hobo.

Sip your red wine. Limiting alcohol is pretty much always advised for people on the electric spectrum. Everyone has a different seizure threshold. French women never drink to get drunk; they savor a glass or two of something sparkling or deep crimson in the face of the crushing anxiety of trying to heal, stay witty, find meaningful work, and support a household. Seeing as how I was always a huge cream-soda fan as a kid, this was a fairly easy swap to make.

Embrace imperfection. So there are still a few vapid, superficial perfectionists in your family and outer circle who immediately assign blame for your appearance and current indeterminate health status. They say things like, "She wasn't taking care of herself or she needs to get more rest" as though I were the cause of my epilepsy and my subsequent asymmetry. The street fighter in me says, "No it's just your dumb DNA, you weenie." Sometimes, a seizure is just a seizure. So let it go. French women never get their elegant knickers in a twist over the small stuff or small people. I would (when back at work again) make a donation to the Epilepsy Foundation in my detractors' names and call it a day. They would get a bit of mail now and then, all while learning a ton about what so many of us with neurological differences deal with day in and day out.

Maintain an air of intrigue. This one was harder for me as I am such a goofball with zero filter, but it was so worthwhile. Simply put: don't give it all up at once. I didn't have to explain what had happened to anyone. I felt explaining would put them at ease, but it's a load of hooey. French women know that withholding selected pieces of information is beguiling. When some douchebag executive bro tried to gaslight me, either I'd have some choice zingers at the ready to make him (or her) feel like a ridiculous asshat while diffusing with humor or I'd have fully mastered my look of mocking indifference with a signature question-mark brow.

Take off one thing before you leave your apartment. Did I really need to bring a rape whistle, mace, and a stun gun with me every time I left the house? The truth is most likely yes, given the shocking normalization of violence in our culture against women, LGBTQ people, immigrants, and the differently abled, but in terms of my own sanity, I needed to chip away at some of the defensiveness I'd been carrying around with me since the diagnosis. Besides, it's much more chic to carry a smaller clutch in the evening or to dispense with the chunky statement necklace so that the dress can shine on its own—sans distraction.

But again, even with all the sage Frenchy wisdom, I still cared about my face, and no amount of me becoming a better person was going to change that. What? It's my face!

16

Gotham Girl, Interrupted

THERE'S A JOKE the famed Russian dissident Masha Gessen often tells: "We thought we had hit rock bottom . . . and then someone knocked from below."

I thought I had hit rock bottom when I broke my mug, but then something else knocked from below. It was big, crazy, feral grief. Grief over everything: my face, a sense of beauty, job, parenting, being a professional patient, and losing Loïc. You name it I was losing it. How was it manifesting itself? As extreme fatigue. It was as if my fears had begun to fossilize as pain across my entire body. In my panicked mind, I wasn't getting better fast enough. It had been four months since the last surgery and there was no bouncing back on the schedule that I, or anyone around me, needed. I still wasn't *myself*.

My friends Arabella and Billie were staying down in Tribeca at this hipster hotel where all the drinks had wrong-sounding finance bro names like the dirty pickle martini and the Moscow tool (served in a penis-shaped copper mug). All the appetizers looked painfully crunchy and gluten free. Billie arrived first. Arabella had arrived on a separate flight and was on her way in from JFK during rush-hour traffic.

It was my first time seeing my friends since the accident. In truth, I'd overprepared and practiced talking so much that by the time I got to the hotel lobby at six that evening, my mouth and the surrounding muscles were already closing for business. The net effect is that my speech sounded vaguely like a deaf person's speech—not that there's anything wrong with that—it's just not what people were used to hearing from me. I still had a shitload of pins and plates holding things together. I needed a Spanx for my face, but I missed these women so much. I had to see them—even as broken as I still was.

It was a warm-ish day in fall, but the subway downtown was still so hyper-air-conditioned, I had to wear a turtleneck. When I walked into the lobby, I immediately spotted Billie at the front desk. She was charming her way into a bigger room—one of her many gifts. She was thanking the desk clerk as I called out to her. She turned and grinned "Jonesy!" Oh, here was someone both fabulously extraordinary and functional and all at once. Could her normalcy just rub off on me for five seconds? It was all I needed, I thought—the sympathetic magic of Billie.

She didn't seem to react to my appearance as much as my words, which were still off-kilter. As we slid into place in the hotel lounge, seats were filling up with gross finance bros. My mouth and gullet felt like an echo chamber with all the vowels bouncing around the inside. I sounded like a sea lion, but I tried to pretend I didn't care. I was just glad to see a friend from home. Arabella was still on her way and texting from the cab, but I knew what she was asking: "Is it really that bad?" and there was Billie texting back in between trips to the loo. "Oh, it's bad!" Not that she was judging, except she was. It's okay. At least she just doesn't do that very New-York-lady-thing, which is *a total trap*. It's when you ask a girlfriend if you should have something done to your forehead, neck, or eyebrows, and she lies to your wrinkly, tired face and says, "I don't even know what you're talking about! Your [fill in body part] looks amazing to me!" Not with Billie. She asks for the truth and she tells the truth. No filter. "Yes, you could do with a thigh lift," she tells you while studying your bare legs and it would mostly be true. Neither she nor Arabella is the type to beat around the bush, and boy if I wasn't the bush right about then. I felt pitied—and it was the worst darkening feeling—seeing them trying to make sense of me for the first time. I could see them renegotiating the angles they had known with the ones that were new. I ordered a "What *She's* Having," which seemed to be just a splash of rosé with club soda and a twist of lemon, and we caught up on the latest West Coast gossip, discussed various divorce proceedings, affairs, and which teenagers had come out to their parents as pansexual—a perfectly reasonable choice. Why cling to binary anything these days?

I tried to maintain an upbeat attitude, but as the night wore on, I could feel myself sinking. I was like a ship with twenty-five-thousand-pound keel, but instead of self-righting, I was just dragging everything down alongside me. I knew going home that night in the cab I was not the same. Nothing was the same. We'd been at Mezzrow, this underground jazz club on West Tenth Street, when I couldn't deny that things with me weren't right. Mezzrow is a place that bills itself more as a "listening room" than a club. Frequently sold out, it really only has a front row and is probably the most intimate venue you'll find in New York City to see and hear amazing musicians. Two eleven-hour reconstructive surgeries and multiple other procedures after my big seizure in the coffee aisle and I still wasn't back to me at all, inside or out. Being there with Arabella and Billie drove this home for me—hard. They were flirting and exuberant and care-free. Both had a way of making friends with the entire world no matter where they went. I wasn't ready for that and I knew it. It was as if I was still wired shut in so many ways.

I walked into my apartment on the Upper West Side, both girls at their dad's, and I despaired. I wasn't going to get better. The seizures would *keep* happening. I would keep breaking things. There were my girlfriends off living their normal, full, rich, kooky, working lives with husbands and vacations and joy and there was me: permanently disfigured, scared, exhausted, jobless, speechless, and joyless. I still felt like I was dying.

This is where little blondes check in . . . now here. I thought. This is my ending, I thought weeping in my kitchen.

I still felt so muzzled. Every waking second, the neuropathy had my face feeling like it was wrapped tight in duct tape. I'd tried to demonstrate the feeling to Ed one night out at dinner by squeezing his chin really hard with both of my hands, and even though Ed is a huge, tough unicorn with a superhero-level threshold for pain, he never tried to pretend to understand: "So, that's what it has felt like all this time? That must be the worst!" To which I'd nodded and said, "Yes, it is!" and explained that this was why it was making me so completely bonkers. I could never ignore my goddamn mug. I'm sure the people in the restaurant thought we were the biggest weirdos, but who cares? This is New York. It's why you move here to begin with. It's the one place on the planet that gives you permission to be exactly as weird as you are because you fit right in with the rest of the marvelous, struggling crazies.

But there were no words for the dark emotional despair I felt that night after seeing Arabella and Billie again except that I knew now that nothing was ever going to be the same for me.

I was always going to be a broken spaz; there was no hiding it. There would never be anymore "passing" as normal or a non-spaz or neurotypical. And I just wanted to sleep through the rest of whatever that meant. So, I did. Or I tried to, except I woke up feeling so bad and so terribly hollowed out. I was buzzing so electric with an aura, I thought I might set the whole building on fire while throwing my guts up beside my bed. With my jaw still growing back together, each hurl felt impossible, like I was having another baby—but this time through my mouth.

Bad, bad, Leroy Brown. Baddest girl in the whole damn town. You might have guessed by now, but I'm naturally a little heavy on the Thanatos. I've always sought to hide my underlying Goth tendencies—the result of the early loss of my one true love, Jim Croce, who died in a plane crash. My fuck account was running so low after so much loss I worried I would have to start giving out IOUs for new ones, that is, "Dear so-and-so, IOU because I totally give a fuck about what you think and what you feel, and so on."

I can't remember who came up with the concept, no doubt some thinker before me like Hannah Arendt, but in this black moment, my despair seemed like the most extreme manifestation of the ordinary. Standing in my kitchen, crying over how one can of coffee and one electric moment had broken my whole life. Looking through old photographs of myself before was a kind of endlessly boring and repetitive exercise whereby I found myself always straining toward the woman I used to be. It felt sadistically futile.

But suddenly you look around your kitchen and your life with its jutting refrigerator and jutting chin and realize everything is destroyed and that nothing will ever be the same. That clarity is terrifying. Your nostalgia for what *was* is so strong it becomes deadly.

There is a peculiar disturbance in the brain, I believe, when something profoundly familiar appears in a strange context. It usually happens right before a breakdown. My everyday world had become so tinted with the dark sheen of despair that my girlfriends' shiny, jubilant normalcy had proven almost too jarring. I had reached a kind of reckoning wherein it all came flooding in, how much I'd lost. Under the surface of things, I had changed irrevocably.

I couldn't risk another seizure there on my own, and I didn't want Arabella and Billie to feel like they had to babysit me on their big weekend in the city. They had tickets for culture and shows and things. Ed was closing up his summer cabin in the Berkshires and Holly had her daughter home from college. I also didn't have enough confidence in my new meds yet to "werewolf" myself on my own. I *had* to go to the ER. I couldn't risk breaking everything all over again.

I WRITE A VERY SNARKY weekly rant called *Gotham Girl*. As part of my trying to get better, I'd started to focus mostly on New York's incandescent weirdos. I love them. I love this city, this capital of neurodiversity, because it's a place that lets all these differently wired people be how they are and it accepts them. This is a place where a nun, a drag queen, and a hard-boiled detective with Tourette's syndrome can all mix it up and usually be fine.

But things were not fine. I had gone into the ER, trying to do the responsible thing because I was worried I was going to have a seizure, and it had all gone sideways. I had said the wrong thing, in the wrong place, at the wrong time, and now I was sitting in a mental hospital with my closest girlfriends.

"What on earth did you say to them, Jonesy?" Billie sat back in her chair and surveyed the expanse of the cinderblock day room in full-on WTF mode.

"I said . . . I didn't necessarily want to spend forty more years having seizures. I don't think that's unreasonable? I was actually trying to do the right thing, and now they won't let me go home."

"Oh, for fuck sake—I'd totally kill myself! It makes perfect sense," Billie proclaimed loudly. The nurse looked over now.

"Not helping!" I whisper-yelled now. "You can't say those kinds of things in here! They take it all very, *very* seriously."

Here they'd both flown back from San Francisco for a big girls' weekend and now I'd gone and ruined it. I spotted their couture through the small wire-hatched window in the door. They were both dressed to the nines in Alexander Wang and Phillip Lim, ready for a big night out. Billie is tall, blonde, and fearless. Her charisma is an unparalleled weapon. She's the Obi-Wan Kenobi of British female charm. Arabella is willowy and fiery with rich, auburn, shoulder-length hair. The cut is always perfect. She has volume without frizz. Her gladiator pumps could kill you in a millisecond—so tall and sharply heeled. She is also one of the most generous people I have ever encountered.

"Besides, my family lives forever," I continued. "I'm the healthiest spaz on the planet."

"Well," Billie said, "I'd be fucking insane if I'd broken everything. Did you tell them you don't actually want to die *right now*?"

"Of course I told them I don't want to die! I went to the ER because I thought I was having another grand mal. I just didn't want to break any more bones, but the doctor there was practically Doogie Howser and twelve. I think I scared him. I doubt if his testicles have even descended yet."

"You sound so . . . *normal*!" Arabella piped up. She was momentarily focused on removing all the individual staples from the stack of *US Weekly*, *People*, and *Vogue* magazines they had brought me. Apparently, tiny staples were not allowed on the psych ward because they could be turned into objects used for self-harm. I had no interest in harming myself. I just wanted to go home.

"I know, right?" I whispered. "I think it's the total fear coupled with the intense muscle relaxants they gave me to prevent the seizure. My face isn't going into lockjaw mode the way it usually does at the end of the day. But there are people here in serious difficulty."

Arabella asked, "Will you be out in time for the opera opening?"

"Um . . . I'm not sure?" Oh God, my girlfriends were party-hopping, psych-ward socialites. How was *I* the one who was locked up again? I'd just wanted sleep and to not spaz again.

I heaved a sigh slouching in my chair. I was never going to get out of here with these two madcap lovelies as my references. They had no idea I was so broken. Or maybe they really *did* and this was exactly what I needed: *not* to be made to feel bad about it. Meanwhile, the nurse was signaling that our time was up.

"Don't get that out," I whispered to Billie. I could see she had stashed some champers in her purse. "We'll be so busted. Look, people who have seizures are often mistaken for having other things—like being junkies or being mentally ill. All I know is that I'm sad. I miss my*self* . . . from before and I don't know if she's coming back."

"ARE YOU *CRAZY*?" I couldn't believe her. I realize now that this was probably an impolitic question to ask a shrink—especially one with a boyfriend reluctant to commit and her twenty-nine-year-old biological clock ticking, and who was already late to Rosh Hashanah. People in New York will tell a mute person everything. The CIA could use me on terrorists and I'd get the evil masterminds to spill every last secret down to what they're getting their favorite auntie for her birthday.

"Ms. Jones, do you currently have thoughts of harming yourself?"

I sighed so hard I could have broken my face all over again. "No. I think there's been a misunderstanding. I just wanted to sleep. I have epilepsy. My last seizure was very bad. I was trying to avert another one by coming into the ER *voluntarily*. If I'd wanted to kill myself, all I would have to do is stay home in my nice, comfy apartment with my books and *not* take any of my antiseizure meds and my brain would take care of things on its own by burning out like a light bulb."

"So, you don't want to die?"

How could I get it across to her? "I don't want to have seizures. I'm homesick for my old face and life, but no, I don't want to die. Just please, go to Rosh Hashanah," I pleaded, exhausted, my right to the truth had been completely revoked.

"What about grief counseling?"

"For what?"

"Your face?"

"Oh." I half thought she was joking. Then I remembered where I was.

"Well, it *is* like a death, isn't it?" She offered.

"Yes, I suppose it is." Oh my God, I thought. That was *exactly* what I needed: a process for mourning the old me. "Can you give me a referral?"

You can see a small spark of happiness in a doctor's eyes when they realize they've solved something, when they've made a small but significant difference. "We'll get you discharged tomorrow morning," she said.

I TOOK MY LOOSE-LEAF celebrity gossip magazines to the TV room where all the other patients were watching *The Bachelor*. There was a vast shortage of reading material on the ward, so I plunked them down on the coffee table for the other inmates, who included a permanently irritated socialite, a schizophrenic philosophy professor, a gangster artist who thought she was Maya Angelou, a fifty-something-year-old teamster guy, and a young bipolar Columbia law student—who made a point of always answering the only phone on the ward. Together we resembled the goofy, misfit cast of a sitcom. I watched as they flocked to the new reading material, sharing sections with pronounced civility. Here was my tribe.

I know there's a great deal of stigma to overcome with mental illness and chronic conditions like epilepsy, but I thought to myself in that moment—and I still believe this—maybe sanity is slightly overrated. I'll take these people on the ward with me. And I'll take Billie and Arabella over bland, ordinary folks any day.

17

DNR

IN A TEACHING HOSPITAL, surgery is like an office party where the backstory is that everyone in the room is up for a promotion. There's music, there's mingling. Everyone is laughing, being witty and charming and on their best behavior for the boss, which in this case was still maxillofacial program head Walter. There's usually *always* one cocky-cad-hot-shot in the mix—handsome but also handy with a scalpel. And you are the guest of honor, who no one really knows that well, the one who is held at the door for check-in, questioning, paper signing, and then suddenly they're drawing on your face with a Sharpie so that they don't cut in the wrong place. They really are *terribly* excited to have someone to cut open. It's a teeny bit creepy.

By the fourth surgery and after a hundred or so smaller procedures, I could spot the fear in their eyes, especially the anesthesiologist. She was a young, dear heart, who still had baby fat and dimples. She looked terrified that she was going to kill me. Lord, that breathing/feeding tube thing up the nose and down the throat was just so Guantánamo. Crikey! But there is a deep fatalism as well as a strident optimism that comes with having anything chronic and spending two years with a doctor—week in and week out. Only in New York would this happen. I ran into Walter in the neighborhood right before my surgery and after another patient's funeral. The patient was a jumper who had committed suicide—successfully this time. Walter was so sad. I don't think I'd ever seen him so down. He kept telling me I needed to eat more, that I was too skinny, and I told him I had just had a burger with my friend Debbi and now I was in pain from yapping with her for three hours. He joked, "So, what'll it be, kid, Motrin or heroin?" This had been the banter of my weekly play date with him. I'd gotten used to it. I'd gotten used to *him*. I looked forward to seeing him and everyone in the office there, the glamorous Anna, the hilarious Marie, and the quietly cunning Christine, always a glint in her eye, because it meant progress, even if slow, even if it meant I had become a professional patient. Optimism over the course of years of multiple surgeries and procedures requires a kind of stubborn, willful innocence, a movie-style suspension of disbelief for a really implausible horror film. Fatalism is practical and sensible. One in five epileptics dies from a seizure. What felt most impractical, most delusional, was to try to keep living if your body and brain were done. What people with chronic conditions like epilepsy live with more than anything is the fear of the B word: burden. No one wants to become a burden or a victim to anyone. The whole point of these years is how to learn *not* to be devastated by every big or little thing that happens to you.

On the table now, I was talking with the surgical nurse, answering her last questions before going under.

"And it says here that you have a DNR—a do-not-resuscitate order?"

"Uh, yeah. If things go south, just let me go off into the universe with the rest of the star stuff."

Walter interrupted, "What do you mean you have a DNR? You don't need a DNR. What, are you depressed?"

"Err, uh, no. I'm mean . . . not today. I just don't want to wake up as a root vegetable and be a burden to people. Is that too much to ask?"

He shook his head. "Well, I won't allow it. *Why* do you need a DNR?"

"I-I was just doing like Suze Orman told me . . ." Suze had been one of our clients and had always preached on the merits of having an advanced medical directive. What can I say? Even if you've heard it before, the woman makes total sense.

"Don't you *want* to live?"

All the residents went quiet. "What about the girls?" he demanded. "What about your dumb dog? And what about Ed? You can't just quit!" I'd never seen him so extraordinarily irritated, so thoroughly Oscar Madison-ish.

"Fine, I'll live. Jesus . . . so touchy."

And we started laughing. And I did. Live, that is.

18

A Love Letter from My Brain

I GOT THIS LETTER from my brain yesterday. The penmanship was atrocious. She must have been drinking. I think she may be under the impression that she is a young Elizabeth Taylor. You can almost picture her staggeringly violet eyes staring you down as she speaks:

Dear Alisa,

My dearest love. Yes, I know it looks like a real mess in here right now and I know my writing you this love letter may seem a bit unorthodox in light of the situation but, darling, I couldn't resist. The temptation in me, across my every axon and dendrite, was too powerful. I know you feel betrayed by me, by my electrical taunts, by what seems like faulty wiring between my lobes, but my love for you is boundless.

It's complicated, but I have evolved and adapted for more than one hundred thousand years across one hundred billion cells to keep you safe, to keep you interesting, and to keep evolving. In truth, I am a secret radical—like Jane Austen or Emily Dickinson. With more than sixty-five million people worldwide living with epilepsy, one in twenty will develop seizures in his or her lifetime.

These people don't need practical, prescriptive advice for surviving life with seizures or a chronic condition. They need to know how to make meaning of seizures, of epilepsy, and of life. I am more of a process than I will ever be a specific organ with a function, and because of that, I am always becoming something new, something else. Writing about seizures is like writing about the soul. It's forever elusive. Every time you think you've captured it, it shifts form or disappears altogether.

While we may indeed have to respect *some* of the cards we've been dealt, we can still recraft the story—to laugh a little. Or a lot. You are never beholden to a shit narrative, my dearest love. Try to take that very same richness and intensity of feeling that comes with this electric condition and apply it to every moment *in between* and ahead.

If you feel you have been on the outside of your life for so long, like an uninvited guest hovering at the periphery, and that you can never claim it back, I am writing to tell you that you are wrong. I, your brain, was wired to write multiple futures. When I send you messages that say, "Stop, go back!"; or, "Don't do this! This is dangerous and it will involve pain"; or, "You will get hurt," I need you to listen and hear me and know that I have evolved over all this time to protect you and to perpetuate your species. Every problem I present you with is an adaptive piece to propel the story. Your story. The one you are writing at this very second. If you learn from these adaptations, if you are obsessed by them, take responsibility for them, and ask yourself why they happened, always why, so as to experience them so deeply that they feel like a gift, then you can forgive yourself for these misadventures and move forward. Then you can heal others, and in so doing, heal yourself.

Now, as your brain, I feel I have a duty to inform you that I have this fantasy that all the nerds and weirdos of the world will read these words here and, bit by bit, even in the reddest, most singular, and closed of rural backwater places and towns, they will grow into radical neurodiverse sleeper cells. Think of them as subversive little tribes of epileptics, autistics, depressives, and other neurotypes all disrupting the stigma. I say this because I want you (and all the differently abled) to experience odd, rare sparks of joy; to be curious about what it means to be electric; and to understand how you can take something that *should* be really, truly awful and rewrite it to reflect joy.

Words can spark such fires, and we are only just learning how to torch the ground rather than ourselves.

Lovingly,
Your brain (the spaz)

19

The New Rules of You

I F SELF-KNOWLEDGE is the key to happiness, then these are the practical things being a spaz has taught me beyond an extreme hatred of yard art and sharp coffee tables. (You only need to hit your head so many times on a garden gnome to know that they serve no purpose for anyone.)

We need playlists—be they music, literature, TV, or movies— to remind us who we are and who we *can* be, to help reinforce our personal myths of self. In my case, I really needed my funny self because my grief needed somewhere to go. I also needed to change my work life considerably, which meant working less, saving more, and learning to live with uncertainty while still making ends meet.

So, when freaking out over hormones or seizures or big professional or personal stress, I decided I needed new rules and to try the following:

Implement the total high-protein, high-fat diet. Drink bacon. Go on a beef cleanse! Once I could really eat again, that's what I did. From steak tartare to a whole prime rib—it actually made me feel so much better. Also, I stopped drinking. Sobriety can be a lark. I actually felt so much better. I had . . . what's it called again? Energy! Instead, opt for lots of sparkly things: cream soda, juice spritzers, and playing Bananagrams with Ed.

Remember your fenced-in area when you're just pissed as hell at white men everywhere and maybe channel rage creatively? Ever thought of macrame? No, not so much. Just remember that emotional regulation is your friend. Channel your rage toward some serious house cleaning. New York is filthy—everything here is covered in a thin coating of feces and takeout grease. Fire the maid and power dust. Throw tampons and pillows, no solid objects or phones, when frustrated. Try a temper tantrum on that Tempur-Pedic. It's actually quite satisfying. Engage in daily exercise at the gym, dance class, or better yet, the park.

Make a chronic illness crisis playlist, meaning find your own macaroni and cheese comfort-food equivalent for movies, TV, and music for postseizure times or any time of big, scary, or chronic stress. What makes comfort TV? Hilarity and smaller, more addressable problems. It's all about escapist entertainment that doesn't make you feel you need a shower afterward. You want media fare that's going to make you feel like you ate an okay amount of mac and cheese—but not too much.

My hard and fast rules for things to steer clear of: No politics. No *Billions*, even though Maggie Siff is a badass! No *Homeland*. No TMZ gossip or reality awfulness. No sad, scary news. No big disasters, nothing with facially oriented fight scenes. Late-night chat shows that are too shouty, angry, or political tend to exhaust this girl, so I pass on those too—as much as I love them during nonseizure, feeling-good, not-so-hormonal days.

Most of all, keep it light. You may feel like ugly-crying but *resist*! My playlist is very weird and very specific to me as it reminds me of who I am and what qualities I'd like to project internally and occasionally around the house. It's all temporary, not-too-thoughtful distraction that says everything is going to be okay in my sometime-tumultuous little world (and lately in the greater world as well). And it's totally girly, so apologies in advance. Listicle dropping . . . now:

Movies

Anything Nancy Meyers writes or directs is always a safe bet when I'm in postseizure mode, although *Something's Gotta Give* with Diane Keaton is a clear winner to my mind. Plus, Diane writes out all of her sadness while boffing Keanu Reeves— which is a good for any writer.

Chick flicks where the heroine runs away are always a good bet. Anything where they eat and drink their way across Tuscany or the French countryside or a quaint English village will do. People write this genre off, but after a big seizure or chronic thing, you need a bit of "gay and away!"

Seems Like Old Times with Goldie Hawn reminds me of my love for dogs and hapless writers. I also relate to being torn between the impulsive allure of Chevy Chase and the steadfast reliability of Charles Grodin. The last shot in the film *so* used to be my face back when I could smile. Plus, Ed always tears up when he sees it, which is sweet.

TV

Bored to Death: There's something about Ted Danson as Graydon Carter teaming up with stuck-writer Jason Schwartzman and comic book artist Zach Galifianakis and running all over New York City that comforts. Maybe it's that they are solving petty crimes and having literary skirmishes that just makes my heart do a tiny dance every time I watch it.

30 Rock: I love its awkward beginnings and then how it evolves into some of the tightest writing you will ever see on broadcast television. The pilot where Liz buys all the hot dogs will make you feel good and also want all the hot dogs. The music cues always lift me too.

The Mary Tyler Moore Show: Loveable icon of feminism. Who doesn't adore her hair—at least in the beginning seasons (volume but no frizz)? And the way she always says "Mr. Grant" is like an operatic vocal hug.

Midsomer Murders: Who wants to have cream tea and solve convoluted but still *totally manageable problems*, with handsome gents in the English countryside? I do! Sign me up! Plus, there are nineteen seasons to watch and then forget, and then watch again!

Pushing Daisies: The greatest TV love story ever told complete with pie and spinster aunties. The vibrant color of the sets is enough to lift my mood on the darkest of days. It's total visual Prozac.

Okay, enough television—you should listen to *Yacht Rock* (cue Michael McDonald and Kenny Loggins) and read more anyway. In the meantime, here are some other new rules of me:

See a trauma coach, not to stir up the past but to reimagine the future. Maybe keep this person on retainer? Again, when about to go down the bad spiral and the chain of total mental anguish, ask yourself, WWNMD? Or What Would Nancy Meyers Do? How would she write this movie? Come prepared with crisp, white shirts and un-oaked Chardonnay. (Not too much, though, alcohol lowers the seizure threshold.)

Get your beauty rest. Sleep is the most important piece of the brain equation—especially when it comes to staying seizure free, so know this: Nora Ephron was right. It *is* that second glass of wine that keeps you up at night, *so don't do it!* No partying with the Plastics as that kind of bullying will rot your insides and give you wrinkles. Know how to tell the good drama from the bad. Drama gets a bad rap, when people shake their heads and say things like, "She's soooooo dramatic." When is drama good? When is it useful? When it propels you into a new way of seeing.

You might end up with an overdeveloped sense of justice. I think it runs in our family. You might feel the need to right many of the world's wrongs in ridiculous and unexpected ways due to a maniacally low tolerance for injustice and petty digs. But here's the thing of it: spoon theory is real. Coined by Christine Miserandino in her 2003 essay "The Spoon Theory," the idea grew out of a conversation in a diner in which a friend asked her what having lupus, a chronic autoimmune disease, felt like. Miserandino grabbed spoons from nearby tables to use as props.

She gave her friend twelve spoons and asked her to recount a typical day, taking a spoon away for each activity she undertook that day. Each spoon, of course, was a finite unit of her own physical and emotional energy and had to be rationed to avoid running out of spoons before the end of the day. The new rule of living with epilepsy is getting real with the fact that I have about four to five spoons in my drawer on any given day. *I decide how to use them.* I can't use them all up on every skirmish—even if my exaggerated sense of what's fair or right or how things should be is telling me to do so. Save your spoons.

That said, your cerebral lights could go out like that at any time, so take nothing for granted. Celebrate every holiday, even the little ones like Arbor Day—yes, national tree day—it's the last Friday of every April, every year. Just don't send paper cards because that defeats the overall purpose of conservancy.

Believe in and support places in the world that adapt to different neurotribes and neurotypes—places like the quaint village of Purley in Great Britain, which has evolved into a dementia-friendly town where if you get lost or forget who you are, a designated someone will make sure to remember for you and get you to a safe place. Glasgow in Scotland has also proclaimed itself a city morphing to better accommodate individuals on the autism spectrum who might be dealing with sensory overload. Leave it to the Estonian police force to provide on-site teddy bears to children involved in traumatic accidents where the parents are hospitalized. That may sound a bit harsh in the current dystopian political climate, but who would say no to such a small comfort to children in momentary crisis? The new rule of you is to ask yourself how you can be more human in fraught, uncertain moments?

Support neuro-specific design. From the airbag helmet to hearing aids that transition into vibrating bracelets for fire safety at night, these innovations are awesome. The round houses with rounded interiors and softer edges that can be 3-D-printed in a matter of days are perfect for different neurotypes. There are whole industries that can be built around neurodiversity, and we need to start reimagining our everyday world to adapt.

Don't be a dick. It's so easy to hop the express train to Dickville. This extends to your various mothers-in-law. It's a universal truth that this will be a fraught relationship, so don't go there; be nice because you'll never win against his/her mother.

That forty-nine-year-old dyspeptic person with rapidly developing man-boobs is still your mother-in-law's baby. Let her reign supreme.

Health insurance company greed will soon manifest as the cruel embodiment of the corporate state in the form of millions of chronically ill, disabled, differently abled people suffering, so we have to look out for each other. Take care of your fellow humans be they spazzy or otherwise. Lovely weirdos can only make us stronger and save the world. Believe it. Find other people who relate to your brand of crazy, but don't hang out with people who are exactly like you as it can feel like hanging out with *only* you and then you both morph into even more of a bummer. I'm just saying there are times you might need some vapid, slightly nefarious people in your life for levity, for diversity, and to show you very starkly what you are not.

When you are super sore from a seizure, you may want to take a bath. A shower can be excruciating with how many muscles are used during a grand mal. Many people will tell you not to do this. For my part, I like to sing in the bath so that whoever is around knows that I'm just fine. If I suddenly stop singing, the person I'm with knows to come in and check on me.

Beware of the third day after a seizure. This has consistently held true throughout my life with epilepsy. By the third day after a seizure (or a baby) you are probably due for a major meltdown, or what I like to call a HORE—short for HOrmonal Rage Event. It may have nothing to do with my hormones, but it helps to remember that the world may not be ending after all and that tomorrow is a new day.

In terms of consistent long-term care, you may need to go on a lot of first dates with different doctors throughout life to get what you need—do it. Remember, you are the boss of your health care. Don't let medical orthodoxy get in the way, and don't wait to start a new treatment if things aren't working for you. If I had pushed harder with my first jerk-neurologist to try the drug I'm on now, I might have been able to avoid breaking my face, jaw, and teeth altogether—but *he* didn't think it was necessary.

Make a spaz kit so that you feel less anxious about being out and about if you have a seizure or any health crisis. What are the things you need in that moment? For everyone it's different. For me it's a combo: baby wipes, fresh knickers, emergency meds, Advil, bandages with the Neosporin built right in, a tiny toothbrush kit, and a talisman. For me, talismans are a mooring type of object that I immediately recognize, such as a photo, a keychain, or lipstick, that reminds of me and who I am. I tend to wake up afraid, so one key object or person is paramount.

Know that you will need to sleep for about two to three days afterward. This sleep will feel like twenty minutes because neurological time travel is exhausting, but this is normal for you.

You will be expected to have wisdom, bromides, and platitudes by your middle age, and it's so totally okay to answer, "I have no fucking clue, but let's figure it out. We don't have to be devastated every time something horrible happens—we can even be funny about it." That said, to smooth out the disarray that life may fall into after a diagnosis of epilepsy or anything seriously chronic, sometimes it helps a little to detach. Seizures have taught me that what the mind refuses to face, the body eventually will. To care for ourselves equips us to better care for our loved ones. And sometimes that means admitting the hard thing—that you're ill, that you only have three spoons left in the drawer, and that getting better may stretch out over the course of a lifetime. I always thought that when you got sick, you either fought it and got better, or you succumbed; but what my seizures have taught me most about the gift of chronic crises is that you come to love the in-betweens so much. I never knew their full worth until now.

EPILOGUE

On Being a Narwhal

How does it always come down to unicorns? I don't know why, but it does. And I don't know why I picked the narwhal—otherwise known as the "unicorn of the sea"—as my spirit animal slash metaphor. It was purely accidental. The beast-word fell out of my mouth during a conversation I had many, many seizures ago, with my younger daughter.

We were talking about surgery as a solution for my seizures. Sophie came with ready opinions. My careless comment was something like, "Yeah, but I'm just not sure I want to be a narwhal. I'm not ready, yet." I'd said in jest. I was not into the idea of lobotomy scars at the age of forty-two, but right then I could see my daughter was absolutely serious about my life and death. A child should never have to worry about her mother is the constant refrain I hear in my head. I realize now that it was a very vain and selfish retort and probably made me a jerk. Because, of course, you would do anything to assure your child that they will never be left on their own. Never be abandoned. But well, I never claimed I wasn't a jerk, so if you assumed I wasn't, that's a tiny bit on you, my lovelies.

In narwhal lore, its name is derived from the Old Norse word *nár*, meaning "corpse," in reference to the animal's greyish, mottled pigmentation, created by the creature's summertime habit of lying still at or near the surface of the sea.

The Inuit oral tradition is rich in legends about transformation. One such legend holds that there once was a woman with beautiful, long hair who was married to a cruel and abusive husband. One day, she was standing beside a river with her hair down when her husband came after her with great violence. Just as he was about to reach her, she fell backward into the water below and sank out of sight. When she emerged at the mouth of the river, she had transformed into a narwhal with a long tusk. Rapids were forming in the river and, because her hair was spread out in all its length, it began to twist around and around in corkscrew fashion—forever safe now from her abusive husband. This was the mythological reason why narwhal tusks are formed with a corkscrew twist. The spiral horn is actually a long tooth and was believed to possess magical curative properties.

The writer Jules Verne suggested the creature sought to run ships through with its tusk. That seems unlikely in that nerves tunneling through the narwhal's tusk, an upper canine tooth that runs seven to ten feet long, suggest that it is actually a sensory organ. It's believed that the animals use it to collect information about their environment and about one another. Male narwhals, for example, may tap or scrape their tusks together as a means of communication. The tusk might also be sensitive to environmental factors, such as water and air pressure, temperature, and chemical cues, thereby facilitating communication and prey detection.

The narwhal lives year round in the Arctic waters around Greenland, Canada, and Russia and can live up to the age of a menopausal lady. They are often killed by suffocation when the sea ice freezes over. Another cause of fatality, specifically among young creatures, is starvation. The current population of the narwhal is about seventy-five thousand, so narwhals, though not technically endangered, are considered a fairly rare species.

Some medieval Europeans believed narwhal tusks to be the horns from the legendary unicorn. As these horns were considered to have magic powers, such as neutralizing poison and curing melancholia, Vikings and other Norse traders were able to sell them for many times their weight in gold. Used for foraging and mating rituals, the tusks were sometimes also crafted into cups that were thought to negate any poison. During the sixteenth century, Queen Elizabeth received a bejeweled narwhal tusk worth more than ten thousand dollars from the renowned adventurer and explorer Sir Humphrey Gilbert, who claimed the tusk was from a sea unicorn. The tusks were considered a staple of various aristocratic cabinets of curiosities at the time, much the same as epileptics.

I'd always held an outlandish view of epilepsy surgery. I pictured a horrifically grotesque procedure with my brain split in half and horn growing out of my forehead. It may have been a lack of vision on my part. Most likely it was that my parents just didn't explain things adequately. Back in the 1970s, it was still common for kids to have their tonsils taken out. If you had repeat cases of tonsillitis or strep throat, pediatricians routinely took them out.

I was a total tonsillitis kid. Until age seven, I practically lived on that horrid Pepto-Bismol-colored amoxicillin liquid that grown-ups always tried to convince you tasted like strawberry Nestle Quik (such blasphemy). It's a wonder I have any intestinal flora left. My parents dreamt up every possible bribe to persuade me to have my tonsils out. They dangled ice cream, Jell-O, and popsicles—all the things hippie kids never got, but I was adamant about keeping my tonsils.

Plus, and I genuinely don't know how I got this idea into my head, but somehow in my little kid logic I truly *believed* that in order for the doctor to take out your tonsils, they had to saw off your head. Indeed, in my version of the presumed events, the doctors and nurses gave you loads of shots (which I was not keen on) to make you fall asleep, during which they cut off your head, removed your tonsils with pliers, and then sewed your head back on like Frankenstein. That was a tonsillectomy in my dark imaginings, and no one could convince me it was worth having my head sawed off.

It didn't even occur to me that all doctors really did was just put some long skinny tongs in your mouth, snip-snipped, and then you woke up for ice cream. Why my parents never explained this to me or probed any deeper into my trepidation remains a mystery.

But this gets me back to the epilepsy surgery, and the other question Sophie put to me when I was in my cyborg headgear, about whether there was an operation that would make my seizures go away forever? I pretty much did the same thing all over again. When it came to a discussion of surgery for my epilepsy, my imagination went straight back into overdrive like it did with my tonsils.

The most common type of epilepsy surgery is called a temporal lobectomy. In this procedure, a very specific, overly electrical, hyperactive part of the brain is removed. The second, less common type of epilepsy surgery interrupts nerve pathways that allow electrical impulses to spread across both the right and left hemispheres of the brain. The term "disconnection" is sometimes used to describe it. This is the kind of surgery I imagined would have me looking like a narwhal with a big horn scar between my eyes, separating my lobes. And I didn't want disconnection inside my brain. If anything, I wanted more understanding outside of it—in the world.

The actual conversation I had with my neurologist about why I wasn't a candidate to have the surgery had to do with the location of my seizures. This was the real issue. There was too great a risk to my language, memory, and my ability to walk. I might be too impaired afterward, and even though my seizures were fierce, they weren't intractable and frequent enough to warrant brain surgery. I didn't know how to explain this to Sophie at the time. I also didn't know how to explain the other risks.

Most neurologists don't like to talk about Sudden Unexpected Death in Epilepsy (SUDEP). It's so important that they do because many people with epilepsy are unaware that there's a possibility of unexpectedly dying from the disorder. While it is an uncommon but fatal complication of epilepsy, it affects one in a thousand adult patients and one in 4,500 children with uncontrolled seizures every year. Many physicians are hesitant to discuss this rare risk of death because they don't want to frighten their patients. Of the participants who completed a 2017 Epilepsy Foundation survey, 100 percent felt that adult patients with epilepsy had a right to be informed about SUDEP, and 92 percent agreed that doctors should be required to disclose that information to them. Additionally, the limited survey showed that 81 percent of patients felt that simply *knowing* about the rare risk of death motivated them to consistently take their medication, and 85 percent said it encouraged them to better manage their seizure triggers—such as sleep, alcohol, and stress. That said, it's also important that we, as people with chronic conditions and disorders like epilepsy, don't get locked into certitudes about it. There is no one narrative for epilepsy or for neurodiversity. Drop the guilt and the shame however you can. Write it off, ride it out, walk it off, and shout it out.

Imagine any number of narrative futures because this is what our brains were designed to do. According to some of the most recent research on how the human brain works, we call our species *Homo sapien* or "wise man," but this is most likely a very poor moniker. We would be more aptly called *Homo prospectus* or *Homo possibilitās* in that our brains are wired to use very different parts of themselves in highly integrated ways to formulate multiple narrative futures for ourselves—collectively and individually. Through the mathematics of space and time, our brains are able to imagine and (sometimes) execute on a wide variety of outcomes and possibilities more so than we are wired to be able to solve or learn from the past. We are, in short, wired for the future, and there is an endless gorgeousness to this idea. A beautiful possible.

But now that I sat there with Sophie all these years later, regarding her worried little face, she said very plainly in response to my careless comment, "But *I* would be a narwhal for you." And inside, my heart just broke, or maybe it grew like the Grinch because I would always be a narwhal for her, for both girls. A big, burly narwhal with an unwieldy tusk, swimming in ever-warming waters, I would always be a narwhal no matter how many surgeries and drug trials I had to go through.

I know she still felt betrayed by me, by epilepsy, but to generalize with wild abandon, we all feel betrayed or wronged by our parents at one point or another in life. I felt wronged by mine primarily because no one had ever mentioned epilepsy as part of our family history. It turns out my grandmother may have dealt with seizures as she aged, but no one ever thought to talk about it. We're still not sure, but what I want, what I hope for, is a more open conversation with my daughters (and theirs one day) about neurodiversity, genetics, new treatments, and what it means to live an "electric" life—to touch the fence, so to speak.

There's something awkwardly outmoded about watching a white, privileged, straight-ish woman flail—even absurdly and unabashedly—through personal, social-practical, and professional foibles and expecting a wholesale transformation at the end. My epiphany is, I suppose, that maybe there are no epiphanies. What is the dark alchemy that can turn your vulnerability, contradiction, abjection, and loneliness into light? Maybe it's that you can't just follow the forensic threads of your emotional, neurological, and genetic life back to their different triggers, sources, and origins; maybe it's that you follow them forward and away from comfortable certainties toward different, uncertain, beautiful outcomes.

I'm still revising this idea, but I believe that certitudes keep our own worlds small, confined, and weighted. Possibility, along with hope, is the invisible currency that enlarges and lightens us. Like gravity, you don't always see possibility or hope, but you know its effects: a book falling, our bodies drooping, even straining against it to stay upright. Possibility and hope won't speak to you in your own simple language, because it isn't something that exists outside of humanity. Possibility and hope are only present because we are. It is wired and evolved into us, the same way the electric, epilepsy, and any number of chronic conditions are wired into us. The beautiful possible lives within us, and it's up to us to nurture it and bring it out into the light.

Possibility is only as consistent and constant as we are. I grasped at certitudes and it made life lesser and smaller. It's during those times when the beautiful possible seems the least practical thing that perhaps we need it the most.

I know I apologized to the girls in advance over both of their goopy little heads, right when they were born. I regret the parent I was not able to be. Sometimes I tried too hard to be their pal. If I had known to take greater care to protect them from the drama of this world and my epilepsy, I would go back and be better for them, for they have been all the joy that I ever need. Their soft, sour-milky breaths, nestled to me, to my chest. If I could protect them from the past, present, and all the different futures, I would have. I will—and will still—try always.

At the same time, I want to tell them wise words from an old friend that "caution is a thief" and not to let it or unwarranted fear take away their eccentricity, their electricity, their neuro-diversity, their innate juiciness, and their spaz sense of adventure, empathy, and compassion. I don't think it ever will. They are bright, fierce girls who know that in dark times, we all have a responsibility not just to our own single light but to *all* the neurodiverse lights twinned in a fugitive mind.

Acknowledgments

Eric Myers, *my friend, agent, and invaluable guide;*
Don Weise, *for working wonders;*
Joy Kimple, *who told me I could;*
Jacqueline Saint Anne, Holly, *and* Mac McKeown—
 tireless cheerleaders and actual lifesavers;
Ned Rust *and* Jim Patterson, *big-hearted, clear-eyed*
 champions;
The Marina Bykova Literary Institute *and the ever-patient*
 Vilma, Carlos, *and* Angel;
dear ones: Alisa *and* Chris Shadix, Mo Malone, Charles
 Albert, Camille Semeniuk, Serena Fritz-Cope, Zach
 Nadler, Marc Blucas, Debbi *and* Jay Baum—*so much*
 gratitude;
Dr. Ira Sturman *and his entire surgical team;*
the teams at Imagine, Charlesbridge, *and* Penguin
 Random House;
Elaine *and* Edwin A. Wiggers, Jr. *for their deep generosity;*
Eric Guichard, *for riling me to action after that one summer*
 in France;
my family *and* friends, *who said I should.*